tea&crumpets

tea&crumpets

RECIPES & RITUALS *from*
EUROPEAN TEAROOMS & CAFÉS

MARGARET M. JOHNSON

Photographs by LEIGH BEISCH & MARGARET M. JOHNSON

CHRONICLE BOOKS
SAN FRANCISCO

Dedication: To my grandchildren, Alec, Will, Robby, and
Lily: I look forward to lots of tea parties together.

Library of Congress Cataloging-in-Publication Data available.

ISBN 978-0-8118-6214-1

Manufactured in China.

Designed by Vanessa Holden
Prop styling by Sara Slavin
Food styling by Dan Becker
Typesetting by Janis Reed

Page 11: Photograph courtesy of The Merrion Hotel, Dublin.
Page 31: Photograph courtesy of The Ritz Hotel, London.
Page 80: Photograph courtesy of Mandeville Hotel, London.
Page 174: Photograph courtesy of The Ritz Hotel, London.
Page 180: Photograph courtesy of The Ritz Hotel, London.

10 9 8 7 6 5 4 3 2 1

Chronicle Books LLC
680 Second Street
San Francisco, California 94107

Acknowledgments

I'D LIKE TO express my thanks to the countless hotels, tearooms, tea salons, and their chefs who contributed recipes for this book. I would also like to acknowledge the support of Tourism Ireland; Visit Britain; Visit Scotland; Visit Wales; Maison de la France; Crystal Cruises; and the Royal Scotsman, an Orient-Express train. Thanks also to Stephen Twining, director of corporate relations, Twinings Tea, for tea history lessons and tips on brewing; to Clearbrook Farms, Astor Chocolates, Andre Prost Company, Walkers Shortbread, and King Arthur Flour for products used in recipe development. To Madeleine Morel, my agent, who continues to provide guidance and encouragement; Bill LeBlond, editorial director, cookbooks, Chronicle Books, for his faith in me again; Amy Treadwell, project editor, Chronicle Books, for her editorial assistance; and to Charles DiPirro, for his assistance with French translations, *merci beaucoup*. Finally, heartfelt thanks to my husband, Carl, for his continued indulgence in me and now tea!

The recipe for Petit Pains au Chocolat (page 147), originally printed in *Bon Appétit*, is used with permission of Rozanne Gold; the recipe for Pierre Hermé's Chocolate-Filled Macarons (page 144), originally printed in *Bon Appétit*, is used with permission of Pierre Hermé; the recipe for Lemon Cream Tartlets with Wild Forest Berries (page 123), originally printed in *The Crystal Cruises Cookbook*, is used with permission of Crystal Cruises; the recipe for Crème Caramel St. Petersburg (page 159), originally printed in *Du Thé Plein la Toque* by Christopher Alary and Pierre Watters, is used with permission of Kusmi Tea.

Introduction

If you are cold, tea will warm you; if you
are too heated, it will cool you; if you are
depressed, it will cheer you; if you are excited,
it will calm you. Thank God for tea! What
would the world do without tea! I am glad
I was not born before tea. ⟶

WILLIAM GLADSTONE, BRITISH PRIME MINISTER

AFTERNOON TEA, that very British tradition where a fondness for tea and a penchant for sweets comes together most agreeably around four o'clock each afternoon, is a not-to-be-missed "event" for any visitor to London. In fact, throughout the British Isles, Ireland, and in many European countries, this pleasurable pause is often the highpoint of the day.

Although the custom of drinking tea dates back to the third millennium B.C. in China, it wasn't until the mid-seventeenth century that tea first appeared in England. The practice of having afternoon tea, however, wasn't established until about 1840, a time when lunch was eaten quite early in the day and dinner wasn't served until eight or nine o'clock in the evening. The story of its creation says that when Anna Maria, the seventh duchess of Bedford (1783 to 1857), was feeling a bit hungry late one afternoon while on summer holiday at Woburn Abbey, she asked her maid to bring tea and a tray of bread-and-butter sandwiches to her room. Anna Maria enjoyed her "taking of tea" so much that she started inviting her friends to join her for this new social event, one that gradually expanded to include assorted fruit breads and small pastries.

Afternoon tea as we know it was born, and before long other hostesses quickly picked up the practice, and elegant tea parties became fashionable social events rather than a meal. Ladies did not go to afternoon tea gatherings to eat but rather to meet their friends, catch up on gossip, chat about the latest fashions and scandals, be seen in the right places among the right people, and, in passing, to drink tea and nibble daintily on a small finger of bread and butter or a little sweet biscuit.

In just a few decades, the custom was well established. During the 1880s, upper-class women would change into long gowns, gloves, and hats for their afternoon tea, which was usually served in the drawing room between four and five o'clock. At first the practice was limited to the upper classes, but it eventually became so popular that tea shops and tearooms began opening for the enjoyment of the general public. Demand for tea wares grew, and soon manufacturers

like Wedgwood, Minton, Royal Doulton, and Royal Albert began producing tea services in fine bone china, trays, three-tiered cake stands, servers, tea caddies, tea strainers, teapots, and tea tables.

Posh hotel dining rooms in London quickly followed the trend, and today places like the Ritz, Savoy, Brown's, and Four Seasons annually vie to be named winner of the "Top London Afternoon Tea Award" presented by the Tea Guild, part of the Tea Council, an organization devoted to raising the profile of tea throughout the United Kingdom. Claridge's, the 2006 winner, has been serving afternoon tea since it opened in 1854, and today it offers a choice of over thirty different types of tea, including the glamorous Royal White-Silver Needles, which is only picked on two days of the year at dawn and then processed entirely by hand.

The Dorchester Hotel, the 2007 winner, prides itself on impeccable service in the elegant surroundings of the Promenade, where discreet piano music plays in the background. Other hotels in the capital continue to impress in the annual tea event—the "Oscar" of the tea world—with "Special Awards of Excellence" presented in 2008 to the Ritz, Goring, Claridge's, Four Seasons, Athenaeum, Chesterfield, and Brown's hotels.

Elegant tearooms are also located at London department stores like Harrods, Fortnum and Mason, and Harvey Nichols, while outside the capital, more modest tearooms like Hazelmere Café in Cumbria, Peacock's Tearoom in Cambridgeshire, Betty's Tea Rooms in North Yorkshire, and Tea on the Green, Essex, are perennial contenders for the Tea Council's "Top Tea Place" honor. The Olde Bakery Tea Shoppe in Winchcombe, Gloucestershire, the 2008 winner, was praised for its "truly special tea experience and perfectly brewed teas."

In addition to the three-course traditional afternoon tea, many places offer Devonshire cream tea (scones and tea only); Champagne tea (three courses along with a glass of premium Champagne); chocolate lover's tea (all chocolate sweets following the sandwiches with "chocolate" Champagne made with Tia Maria and Kahlúa); and all-strawberry springtime teas. In London, many establishments offer themed teas honoring special events, such as the Chelsea and Hampton Court Flower Shows, that feature items like rose-scented macaroons, orange blossom scones, and cheesecake with edible frosted flowers.

But the British are not the only ones who enjoy this lovely ritual, and in many European capitals some of the top names on a "where-to-eat" list are tea salons, cafés, pâtisseries, and confectioneries where tea is served. In Paris, for example, the French enjoy *le goûter*—a cup of tea and a little sweet to tide them over until dinner—at *salons de thé* such as Ladurée, Fauchon, and Mariage Frères, which are renowned for elegant service, crisp macaroons, and buttery madeleines.

In Le Jardin d'Hiver at Le Meurice Hotel, one can also experience the complete ritual of English afternoon tea in the heart of Paris.

Following the sandwiches and scones, one indulges in seasonal tarts, marbled vanilla-chocolate cakes, chocolate fondants, and traditional French *financiers, cannelés,* and madeleines. And while tea is the drink of choice here, *chocolat chaud* (hot chocolate) prepared pâtisserie-style—a blend of chocolate ganache, fresh cream, and milk—is also popular.

Tea & Crumpets will transport you to many legendary European tearooms and storied salons and offer simplified recipes for re-creating, at home, the sandwiches, pastries, cakes, and confections that have made them famous.

Savor the Ritz's cucumber sandwiches, the aristocrat of the tea table, and Claridge's raisin and apple scones. Learn how the chef at Edinburgh's Balmoral Hotel creates the chocolate scones that grace

A proper afternoon tea—this from Dublin's Merrion Hotel—is served on a three-tiered stand with sandwiches scones, and pastries.

its afternoon tea menu, and delight in making banana-chocolate charlottes like those served at London's Savoy.

Be prepared to wow guests by serving teatime specialties like Battenberg cake, a pink-and-white-checkered cake filled with apricot jam and covered with marzipan; Dundee cake, a Scottish fruitcake made famous in the city where marmalade got its start; and French temptations such as *petit pains au chocolate*, chocolate-hazelnut *pots de crème, macarons,* and tea-infused madeleines.

Perfect for armchair travelers, food tourists, intrepid gastronomes, and inventive hostesses, *Tea & Crumpets* will provide both a delicious culinary and cultural experience and a treasure trove of recipes for hosting your own special-occasion afternoon tea. *Bon appétit* and *bon voyage!*

CHAPTER ONE

From Leaf to Cup:
A Little History of Tea

Antique tea tins, like these from Liptons, are part of the fascinating exhibits at the Bramah Museum of Tea and Coffee in London.

I am a hardened and shameless tea drinker,
who for twenty years diluted his meals with
only the infusion of the fascinating plant;
who with tea amused the evening, with
tea solaced the midnight, and with tea
welcomed the morning.

SAMUEL JOHNSON, ENGLISH ESSAYIST AND BIOGRAPHER

THE STORY OF TEA begins in China. According to legend, in 2737 B.C., the Chinese emperor Shen Nung was sitting under a tree while his servant boiled drinking water. When some leaves from the *Camellia sinensis* tree blew into the water, Shen Nung, a renowned herbalist, decided to try the infusion his servant had accidentally created. The resulting drink was what we now call "tea." Whether the story is true or not, tea drinking was established in China many centuries before it made its way to the West.

In the latter half of the sixteenth century, there were a few brief mentions of tea as a drink among Europeans, mostly from Portuguese who were living in the East as traders and missionaries. Although some of these individuals may have brought back samples of tea to their native country, it was not the Portuguese who were the first to ship back tea as a commercial import.

It was, instead, the Dutch, who in the last years of the sixteenth century began to encroach on Portuguese trading routes in the East. By the turn of the century, they had established a trading post on the island of Java, from which the first consignment of tea was shipped from China to Holland in

1606. Tea soon became a fashionable drink among the Dutch, and teapots were among the articles of porcelain imported into Europe from China in ever-increasing quantities during the seventeenth century.

From Holland, tea importation spread to other countries in continental Europe, but it was not officially introduced to England until 1662 by way of the marriage of Charles II to Catherine of Braganza, a Portuguese princess who adored the drink. It was her love of tea that established it as a fashionable beverage, first at court, and then among the wealthy classes as a whole. Capitalizing on this, the East India Company began to import tea into Britain, and its first order, in 1664, was for one hundred pounds of China tea to be shipped from Java.

The British took to tea with an enthusiasm that continues to the present day. It became a popular drink in coffeehouses as well, which

A sign at the Bramah Museum in London points the way to its exhibition featuring Chinese teas.

were locations as much for the transaction of business as for relaxation or pleasure. Only middle- and upper-class men frequented coffeehouses (women drank tea in their own homes), and tea was still too expensive to be widespread among the working class. In part, its high price was due to a punitive system of taxation.

One unforeseen consequence of the taxation of tea was the growth of methods to avoid it, namely smuggling and adulteration. By the eighteenth century, many Britons wanted to drink tea but could not afford the high prices. By 1784, the government realized that heavy tea taxation was creating more problems than it was worth. The new prime minister, William Pitt the Younger, slashed the tax from 119 percent to 12.5 percent and suddenly legal tea was affordable. Smuggling stopped virtually overnight, and this marked the beginning of tea drinking as part of everyday life.

By the eighteenth century, China tea and tea ware were a feature of every aristocratic and middle-class English home. Tea was soon recognized as an invaluable drink for the workforces of the Industrial Revolution, and since it was now cheap and also nonalcoholic, it provided needed sustenance when it was mixed with milk and sugar for people working long hours in factories.

By the nineteenth century, the immense popularity of tea in Britain caused an imbalance of trade with China, and the East India Company began to pay for its tea with opium grown in India and smuggled to China in clipper ships. When this trade was curtailed by the Opium Wars between Britain and China (1839 to 1842), the East India Company acted on an earlier recommendation that it would be possible to grow

Tea ware, like this combination china pot and cup, is a favorite souvenir for visitors to London.

tea in northeast India. In fact, tea had been growing wild there in Assam, but until 1815 nobody knew of its existence.

Indian tea could be harvested over a longer season than the Chinese and Japanese varieties, and British planters introduced mechanized production that was more efficient than the traditional methods. Trade with China began falling, and the British palate adapted to the richer, more malty Indian tea. Tea was also grown in Africa and Ceylon (Sri Lanka) from the late nineteenth century.

Tea is now grown in nearly fifty countries worldwide from Argentina and Brazil to Mozambique and Kenya. The tea bush thrives in mountainous regions bordering the tropics, and it can grow at heights of up to 7,000 feet above sea level. India, particularly its Assam region, is the world's largest producer and exporter of tea. Assam teas are robust with a smooth malt taste. Darjeeling, with tea gardens in the foothills of the Himalayas, produces smaller crops of excellent quality, and with its unique "muscatel" wine flavor, it's ideal as a complement to dinner or for afternoon tea.

Ceylon, now Sri Lanka, produces tea still referred to as Ceylon. The best-quality teas are "high grown" on slopes above 4,000 feet. Ceylon teas are strong but delicate, with a slight bitterness. Kenya now grows some of the very best teas in the world, some nearly 7,000 feet above sea level. These teas are brightly colored with a delicious aroma.

China remains famous for its distinctive black, green, and oolong teas. Lapsang Souchong has a distinctive smoky taste acquired through drying over pinewood fires. Keemun, the traditional tea of old Imperial China, is known for its orchid aroma

Costumed waiters serve afternoon tea in the Palm Court on Crystal Cruise Lines' Symphony and Serenity.

and brilliant red liquor. It is frequently used as the base for scented blends, the most popular of which is Earl Grey, scented with oil of bergamot.

Tea leaves are processed into three main types: black, green, and oolong. Black tea is most popular worldwide, accounting for 77 percent of the world's production. If the leaves undergo the full fermentation process, they become black tea. If the leaves are dried quickly without fermentation, they become green teas, which are highly favored by the Chinese and Japanese and increasingly popular in the West because of their health benefits. Green teas represent 21 percent of the world's production. Oolong tea is semifermented, falling between black and green. The most famous, Formosa oolong, originates in Taiwan (formerly Formosa Island) and has a unique peachy flavor. Oolong teas account for 2 percent of the world's production.

An essential element of modern tea drinking began in 1904 when New York coffee and tea merchant Thomas Sullivan started sending tea blend samples to his customers in hand-sewn muslin bags, thus creating the first tea bags. While there was initial resistance to the idea, it

Three-hundred-year-old Twinings is the official supplier of teas to England's royal household.

would be hard now for most tea drinkers to imagine life without the bags.

Such is the enthusiasm for tea in the United Kingdom that even after the dismantling of the Empire, British companies continue to play a leading role in the world's tea trade, and British brands dominate the world market. Three-hundred-year-old Twinings, for example, is the world's leading premium brand of tea, loose and in bags. In 1837, Queen Victoria granted Twinings its first Royal Warrant, an honor that made them the official supplier of teas to her household, and the company has continued to supply every successive British monarch with their teas.

With recent scientific research indicating that tea drinking may have direct health benefits—findings indicate the components of the tea plant prevent some cancers, reduce the risk of heart attack and stroke, and even lower blood pressure and LDL cholesterol—it is assured that for centuries to come a nice cup of tea will always be a welcome drink.

Top-hatted doorman welcomes guests to Claridge's Hotel, Brook Street, London, where afternoon tea has been served since 1854.

Sandwiches & Savories

*Antique teacups and saucers line the stalls at London's Portobello Market,
one of the most famous street markets in the world.*

There are few hours in life more agreeable than the hour dedicated to the ceremony known as afternoon tea.

HENRY JAMES, ENGLISH NOVELIST

TEA SANDWICHES are the first course for any proper afternoon tea. This tea staple comes in all shapes and sizes, with fillings as simple as a few sprigs of watercress and egg mayonnaise layered on white, wheat, or granary bread (multigrain), or as elaborate as salmon mousse layered with smoked salmon arranged on perfect bread triangles. Sandwiches can be cut into delicate rounds shaped from plain or fluted biscuit cutters, rolled pinwheel style, or served open faced. Official "recipes" for such apparently simple assemblies seem unnecessary, but once you see these delicious sandwich ideas from some of the world's best tearooms, you'll be delighted to serve them at your next afternoon tea.

Here are some tips for creating perfect tea sandwiches. Choose the best-quality firm-textured bread you can buy—white, wheat, rye, pumpernickel, or granary—and cut off the crusts. Small white or wheat rolls also make nice tea sandwiches, and if you have access to artisan breads flavored with ingredients like sun-dried tomatoes, spinach, or olives, use them with simple fillings. Have butter and cream cheese at room temperature for smooth spreading and spread only one side of each slice of bread. Spread the filling evenly but thinly to the edges and corners. Once filled, wrap the sandwiches in plastic wrap, aluminum foil, or cover with a slightly dampened cloth and refrigerate. Do not make the sandwiches too far in advance of serving if the filling is very moist.

And now for the tea. The brewing of the tea is very important. This is the recommended procedure: Fill a kettle to the required level with freshly drawn water and bring it to a boil. Do not reuse boiled water or top up a partly filled kettle. This deoxygenated water has an adverse effect on brewing. Heat an earthenware or china teapot by rinsing it with the boiling water (stainless-steel pots tend to taint the brew). Use one teaspoonful of loose tea per person plus one for the pot. When using tea bags, use one per person. Take the teapot to the kettle and pour freshly boiling water over the leaves. Let sit for approximately 2 to 3 minutes and stir. When using loose tea, pour the tea through a fine-mesh strainer into the teacups.

The wonderful assortment of fine teas available today comes from three main types: black, oolong or red, and green tea. Assam, Ceylon, China Caravan, Darjeeling, Earl Grey, English Breakfast, Irish Breakfast, Irish Afternoon, Keemun, Kenya, Lapsang Souchong, Nilgiri, Orange Pekoe, Rose Pouchong, Russian, and Yunnan are black teas. Formosa/China Oolong and Formosa/China Pouchong are oolong or red teas, and Gunpowder and Jasmine are green teas. At one time, loose tea with its large leaves had a superior flavor as tea bags were made with broken tea leaves and siftings that produced a stronger, darker tea. This is no longer the case, since fine-quality tea bags are now widely available.

While British companies dominate the world tea market—in addition to 300-year-old Twinings, Jackson's of Piccadilly, and Harrogate are well-known brands—tea drinkers in Scotland might favor national brands from blenders such as Brodies of Edinburgh and Brooke Bond; tea drinkers in Wales enjoy Murroughs Welsh blend; and Bewley's, Barry's, and Lyons teas are the most popular brands in Ireland. In France, which is not generally regarded as a tea-drinking nation and never developed fixed traditions regarding tea, people drink the widest variety of teas in the world because they're open to new flavors, blends, and varieties. The French art of tea is explored in chapter five.

Spiced Egg Sandwiches

The Clarence (6–8 Wellington Quay) is one of Dublin's best-located boutique hotels. Situated in the busy Temple Bar area adjacent to the River Liffey, owners Bono and The Edge of the Irish rock group U2 have created a hotel that's very much a reflection of twenty-first-century Ireland. Reflecting that modern spirit, the Tea Room at the Clarence occupies a light, spacious room with a soaring, coved ceiling and sleek contemporary furnishings. Meals served there, including afternoon tea, are straightforward but innovative. Called "egg mayonnaise" in the U.K. and Ireland, this egg salad filling for tea sandwiches is enlivened with curry and chutney—a cooked blend of fruit, vinegar, sugar, herbs, and spice.

4 hard-boiled eggs, peeled

2 tablespoons mayonnaise

¼ teaspoon curry powder

1 teaspoon Major Grey's chutney (see Resources, page 170)

½ teaspoon finely grated lemon zest

12 slices whole grain or multigrain bread, crusts removed (see Note)

In a medium bowl, mash the eggs. Stir in the mayonnaise, curry powder, chutney, and lemon zest until smooth. Spread the egg mayonnaise on one side of each of 6 slices of bread and cover with the remaining slices. Cut each sandwich in half diagonally into 2 triangles. Cover with a damp tea towel or paper towels until ready to serve.

MAKES 12 SANDWICH HALVES

NOTE Try Pepperidge Farm 12-grain bread (from its Farmhouse bread collection) for these sandwiches.

Cucumber Sandwiches

Claridge's Hotel (Brook Street, Mayfair) is one of London's most storied and prestigious hotels. In 2006, the U.K. Tea Guild declared it the winner of its "Top Afternoon Tea Award," the "Oscar" of the tea world. The Foyer is the perfect setting for afternoon teas—traditional or with Dom Pérignon—and it's served while a pianist and violinist entertain. Like other tea salons, Claridge's offers cucumber and cream cheese sandwiches, generally referred to as the "aristocrat of the tea table," with rocket (arugula), although other toppings such as hard-boiled eggs, mint, and tomato relish make flavorful additions.

1 English cucumber, peeled and thinly sliced

Salt for sprinkling

Distilled white vinegar for sprinkling

4 ounces softened or whipped cream cheese

12 slices firm white bread, crusts removed (see Note)

Arugula or watercress sprigs

Put the cucumber slices in a colander and sprinkle them with salt and vinegar. Toss gently to coat the slices. Let sit for 30 minutes to drain excess moisture. Blot the cucumber slices with paper towels. Spread the cream cheese on one side of each of 6 slices of the bread, then top each with the cucumber slices and arugula. Cover each with a remaining slice of bread. Press firmly and cut each sandwich in half crosswise. Cover with a damp tea towel or paper towels until ready to serve.

MAKES 12 SANDWICH HALVES

NOTE Pepperidge Farm or Arnold brand premium white bread is best for these sandwiches.

Salmon Mousse Pinwheels

The Ritz London (150 Piccadilly), conceived and founded by hotelier César Ritz, opened its doors on May 24, 1906. The first steel-framed building of any significance in London—with French chateau-style architecture and Louis XVI interiors—the hotel was, according to Ritz, "a small house to which I am proud to see my name attached." After recently being restored to its original glory, the landmark hotel continues to be one of London's most fashionable addresses for afternoon tea and *the* place to enjoy "Putting on The Ritz." A long-standing recipe for a tea sandwich in the Palm Court is a smoked salmon sandwich served with a whisky-spiked mousse, but this simple, equally delicious version substitutes horseradish and chives for the whisky. You can add a few capers for zing, if you like, and then roll the sandwiches into pinwheels.

SALMON MOUSSE

4 ounces cream cheese,
at room temperature

2 tablespoons unsalted butter,
at room temperature

1 tablespoon minced fresh chives

1 tablespoon prepared horseradish

4 ounces smoked salmon

1½ tablespoons fresh lemon juice

½ teaspoon ground white pepper

1 tablespoon drained capers (optional)

SANDWICHES

12 slices dark wheat or pumpernickel bread, crusts removed (see Note)

2 ounces smoked salmon, cut into thin strips

TO MAKE THE MOUSSE Put the cream cheese, butter, chives, horseradish, salmon, lemon juice, and pepper in a food processor and process for 20 to 30 seconds, or until smooth. Stir in the capers, if using. (Cover and refrigerate for up to 2 days; bring to room temperature for spreading.)

continued

TO MAKE THE SANDWICHES Roll the bread slices flat with a rolling pin. Spread the salmon mousse on one side of each slice and arrange pieces of smoked salmon on top. Roll up and place seam side down on a serving plate. Cover with a damp tea towel or paper towels until ready to serve. Serve pinwheels whole or cut each one in half crosswise and on a diagonal, and serve angled side up.

MAKES 12 LARGE OR 24 MINI PINWHEELS

NOTE Arnold brand German dark wheat bread (from its Whole Grains bread collection) makes delicious pinwheels.

Roast Beef Sandwiches with Horseradish Cream

The Savoy (Strand, West End) is another legendary London hotel. This landmark opened in 1889 and is still a favorite of supermodels, pop stars, and celebrities. As would be expected from a hotel whose first chef was the famous Auguste Escoffier, "taking tea at the Savoy" in its elegant Thames Foyer is truly an event. A mouthwatering array of sandwiches—including this very British roast beef sandwich topped with horse-radish cream—is served on flawless china in the room where Noel Coward performed, Caruso sang, and Pavlova danced in cabaret.

¼ cup mayonnaise or Crème Fraîche (see Note)	12 slices white bread, crusts removed
1 tablespoon prepared horseradish	6 slices rare roast beef
1 teaspoon whole-grain mustard	Salt
	Freshly ground pepper

In a small bowl, whisk together the mayonnaise, horseradish, and mustard. Spread the horse-radish cream on one side of each of 6 slices of bread. Arrange slices of roast beef on top, sprinkle with salt and pepper to taste, and cover with the remaining slices of bread. Press firmly and cut each sandwich in half diagonally into 2 triangles. Cover with a damp tea towel or paper towels until ready to serve.

MAKES 12 SANDWICH HALVES

NOTE To make Crème Fraîche, combine 1 cup heavy whipping cream (not ultrapasteurized) and 2 tablespoons buttermilk in a glass jar. Cover and let stand at room temperature (about 70°F) for 8 to 24 hours, or until very thick. Stir well and refrigerate for up to 10 days. Crème fraîche is also widely available in supermarkets.

MAKES 1¼ CUPS

AFTERNOON OR HIGH TEA? THERE *IS* A DIFFERENCE.

THE TERMS "afternoon tea" and "high tea" are often confused, although in the past, they were actually a peek into your social standing. Afternoon tea originated as a small elegant meal served between a light lunch and late dinner—usually between 3 and 5 P.M.—and mainly a practice of the aristocracy, who enjoyed a leisurely lifestyle. Afternoon tea cuisine eventually expanded to include wafer-thin, crustless sandwiches, shrimp or fish pâtés, toasted breads with jams, and regional pastries such as scones and crumpets. Regardless of the menu, the emphasis was always on presentation and conversation.

The Ritz Hotel is one of London's most storied venues for afternoon tea, served in five seatings daily.

High tea, on the other hand, has always been a more substantial meal, often including sausages or meat pies, and was really an early dinner more suited to the middle and lower classes after a long day at work. High tea (sometimes called meat tea) was the main meal of the day for the working classes and consisted of dinner items such as roast beef, mashed potatoes, peas, and, of course, tea. Today, however, even posh hotel dining rooms like the Dorchester in London are serving high tea as an extension of afternoon tea, offering dishes such as cheese croquettes, chicken liver salad, poached salmon, crab cannelloni, and Scotch eggs.

Chicken Sandwiches with Lemon-Tarragon Mayonnaise

Many London hotel dining rooms subscribe to the theory that there is no need for a sandwich recipe *per se*, as quality ingredients and good bread make a good sandwich, and a good sandwich complements the tea being served. At Claridge's (Brook Street, Mayfair), traditional sandwiches are made with simple ingredients such as ham with whole-grain mustard and watercress, cucumber and cream cheese, egg mayonnaise with watercress, and chicken topped with a lemon-tarragon mayonnaise similar to this recipe.

¼ cup mayonnaise	6 slices cooked chicken
1½ tablespoons fresh lemon juice	Salt
1 teaspoon grated lemon zest	Freshly ground pepper
1 teaspoon dried tarragon	Handful of baby greens
12 slices white bread, crusts removed	

In a small bowl, whisk together the mayonnaise, lemon juice and zest, and tarragon. Spread the mayonnaise on one side of each of 6 slices of the bread. Arrange slices of chicken on top, sprinkle with salt and pepper to taste, and top with the baby greens. Cover with the remaining slices of bread. Press firmly and cut each sandwich in half crosswise. Cover with a damp tea towel or paper towels until ready to serve.

MAKES 12 SANDWICH HALVES

Coronation Chicken

In a small bowl, whisk together ¼ cup mayonnaise, 1 teaspoon mild curry powder and 1 teaspoon fresh lemon juice. Stir in 1 tablespoon mango chutney, 1 tablespoon chopped golden raisins, 1 tablespoon chopped slivered almonds, and salt and freshly ground pepper to taste. Proceed as directed, substituting the curried chutney mayonnaise for the lemon-tarragon mayonnaise.

Chicken, Tomato, and Bacon Sandwiches with Avocado Mayonnaise

In a small bowl, mash the meat from 1 avocado. Whisk in ¼ cup mayonnaise, 1 tablespoon fresh lemon juice, and salt and pepper to taste. Proceed as directed, substituting the avocado mayonnaise for the lemon-tarragon mayonnaise and topping the chicken with a slice of bacon and a slice of tomato.

Chicken, Walnut, and Stilton Sandwiches

In a small bowl, whisk together 1 tablespoon white wine vinegar, 1 teaspoon Dijon mustard, and 4 tablespoons extra-virgin olive oil. Toss with the mixed greens. Proceed as directed, omitting the tarragon mayonnaise and topping the chicken with the greens, a slice of ripe Stilton cheese, and some chopped walnuts.

Leek and Stilton Tartlets

The Dorchester Hotel (Park Lane), the 2007 winner of the U.K. Tea Guild's "Top Afternoon Tea Award," has remained a pinnacle of luxury for more than a half century. Situated between Marble Arch and Hyde Park Corner in London's Mayfair district, the Promenade, recently refurbished by French architect–interior designer Thierry Despont, is the setting for its legendary afternoon tea. While sandwiches always assume center stage for the first course, the Dorchester also offers high tea (see page 31), which sometimes includes savory tarts such as these (adapted here) made with leeks, Stilton (England's "King of Cheeses"), and homemade pastry. Frozen puff pastry is a good alternative.

1 sheet frozen puff pastry (from a 17-ounce package), such as Pepperidge Farm brand	¾ cup chopped leek; about 1 leek, white and pale green parts
1 large egg	2 tablespoons vegetable stock
⅔ cup heavy whipping cream	3 ounces Stilton cheese, grated
1 tablespoon canola oil	Freshly ground pepper

Preheat the oven to 400°F. Line a baking sheet with parchment paper.

Thaw the pastry at room temperature for 40 minutes. Unfold the pastry sheet onto a lightly floured surface. Cut into 3 strips along the fold marks, then cut each strip crosswise into 4 pieces. Place the pastry pieces 1 inch apart on the prepared sheet and score each one ¼ inch in from each side of the pastry. With a fork, prick the center of each several times. In a small bowl, whisk the egg and cream together and brush the pastry edges with some of the mixture. Reserve the remaining egg mixture.

In a medium skillet over medium heat, heat the oil. Add the leek and cook for 3 to 5 minutes, or until soft but not browned. Add the vegetable stock, reduce the heat, and simmer for 5 minutes longer. Remove from the heat and drain all the liquid. Transfer the leek to a bowl and stir in the cheese. Season with pepper to taste, then stir in the reserved egg mixture. Fill the center of each pastry piece with the leek mixture, spreading it within the scored lines (edges will puff to create a crust). Bake for 20 to 25 minutes, or until the mixture is set and the pastry is golden.

MAKES 12 TARTLETS

Goat Cheese and Fig Sandwiches on Raisin Bread

The Four Seasons Hotel (Simmonscourt Road) is a relatively new addition to Dublin's hotel scene, but it has quickly become one of the most distinguished addresses in town. Located in leafy Ballsbridge near the Royal Dublin Showgrounds and the American embassy, the hotel brings the style of the renowned hotel group to the Georgian capital, and along with it, the Four Season's reputation for exemplary dining. Its afternoon tea service, served in the Lobby Lounge, includes this lovely fruit and cheese sandwich (adapted here) made with raisin bread.

FIG SPREAD	SANDWICHES
1 package (10 ounces) dried Calimyrna figs, stemmed and chopped	12 slices raisin bread
1¾ cups water	Two 4-ounce logs plain goat cheese, at room temperature
3 tablespoons sugar	2 tablespoons milk
1 tablespoon fresh lemon juice	Fresh chive sprigs, cut into ½-inch pieces, for topping

TO MAKE THE SPREAD In a medium saucepan over medium heat, combine the figs, 1½ cups of the water, and the sugar. Bring to a boil, then reduce the heat and simmer, covered, for 20 to 25 minutes, or until most of the liquid has evaporated and the figs are nearly tender when pierced with a fork. Transfer the mixture to a food processor, add the lemon juice, and process for 20 to 30 seconds or until smooth (adding the remaining ¼ cup water if the mixture is too thick). Transfer the puréed figs to a bowl. You should have about 1¾ cups.

continued

TO MAKE THE SANDWICHES Preheat the broiler. With a 2-inch biscuit cutter, cut out a round from each slice of bread. Arrange the rounds on a baking sheet and toast them under the broiler for 2 to 3 minutes on each side, or until lightly browned.

In a small bowl or food processor, combine the goat cheese and milk. Whisk until smooth. Spoon the mixture into a piping bag fitted with a star tip and pipe the cheese onto each round of bread. Top with a tablespoon of the fig spread and garnish with 2 pieces of chive. Store remaining fig spread refrigerated for up to 1 month.

MAKES 12 SANDWICHES

THOMAS TWINING founded his eponymous tea company—now the world's leading brand of premium tea—in 1706 when he bought Tom's Coffee House on London's Strand. The area straddled the border between Westminster and the City of London and was newly populated with the aristocracy. Coffeehouses were a popular feature of London life at the time, and competition for business was stiff. Because Twining had earlier been involved in the burgeoning English tea trade, he decided to start selling tea from his coffeehouse with the idea that the drink had great potential.

Despite efforts to repress tea drinking through punitive taxes, tea became increasingly fashionable, especially among the upper classes. Women, in particular, were beginning to enjoy the drink, but the custom of the day excluded them from coffeehouses. Twining

Stephen Twining, director of corporate relations for his namesake company, happily talks tea at their shop in London.

was fast building a reputation for selling only the finest teas—teas that well-heeled London ladies were eager to serve in their drawing rooms—so he began to sell them to women who had their footmen go into the shop while they waited in their carriages outside.

With success came expansion, and by 1717, Thomas Twining had acquired three adjacent houses and converted them to a shop. It is this house, now 216 Strand, that is the site of the famous Twinings shop, which still sells a huge selection of teas, teapots, cups, memorabilia, biscuits, chocolates, and even some coffee. In 1837, Queen Victoria granted Twinings its first Royal Warrant for tea and appointed Twinings as supplier of teas to the household. The company has had the honor of supplying every successive monarch to date.

Earl Grey Croûtes with Creamed Brie

From the late eighteenth century, the Grove (Chandler's Cross, Hertfordshire) has been one of England's most fashionable country homes. In fact, the "weekend in the country" concept was more or less invented at the Grove, with Queen Victoria, Edward VII, and Horace Walpole counted as regular Saturday to Monday visitors. In 1996, the Grove was restored and converted into a luxury hotel, keeping the "weekend in the country" idea very much alive. It's the perfect destination for leisure pursuits, including afternoon tea, which might include this Earl Grey–flavored bread piped with creamed Brie.

BREAD	
¾ cup water	⅓ cup olive oil
3 Earl Grey tea bags	Sea salt
3 cups all-purpose flour	Freshly ground black pepper
2 tablespoons sugar	
1 envelope rapid rise yeast	**CREAMED BRIE**
1¼ teaspoons salt	5 ounces ripe Brie
3 tablespoons butter, cut into pieces	¼ cup Crème Fraîche (see Note, page 30)
1 large egg	Fresh chervil sprigs for garnish

TO MAKE THE BREAD In a small saucepan, bring the water to a boil, add the tea bags, turn off the heat, and let steep for 10 minutes. With a spoon, press on the tea bags to extract maximum flavor. Discard the teabags. Set aside.

In a food processor fitted with a dough blade, put the flour, sugar, yeast, and salt. Process 5 to 10 seconds, or until combined. Add the butter and egg and process for 20 to 30 seconds, or until blended. Reheat the tea to 120° to 130°F and slowly pour it through the feed tube with the machine running. Process for 10 to 15 seconds longer, or until the dough forms a ball. Continue processing for 60 seconds to knead the dough. Transfer the dough to a lightly floured surface, cover, and let rest for 10 minutes.

Roll the dough into a 12-by-7-inch rectangle. Beginning at one short end, roll up the dough tightly like a jelly roll. Pinch the seam and ends to seal. Place seam-side down in a well-oiled 9-by-5-by-3-inch loaf pan. Cover and let rise in a warm, draft-free place for 30 to 45 minutes, or until doubled in size.

Preheat the oven to 375°F. Bake the bread for 30 to 33 minutes, or until the top is golden. Remove from the oven and invert the bread onto a wire rack to cool completely. When cool, wrap in aluminum foil and let rest for at least a day.

Preheat the oven to 375°F. Brush a baking sheet with olive oil.

Cut the bread into twelve ¼-inch-thick slices. With a 3-inch biscuit cutter, cut each slice into a round. Brush the tops of the rounds with olive oil and sprinkle with salt and pepper. Bake the rounds for 5 to 6 minutes, or until lightly browned. Remove from the oven and let cool on a wire rack for about 5 minutes.

TO MAKE THE CREAMED BRIE Put the Brie and crème fraîche in the bowl of a food processor and process for 5 to 10 seconds, or until smooth. Transfer to a piping bag fitted with a plain tip and refrigerate for 1 hour.

Pipe the Brie onto the croûtes and garnish with sprigs of chervil.

MAKES 12 SANDWICHES

Truffled Wild Mushroom Tartlets

Quiche-like tartlets are a delicious complement to the sandwich course and, luckily, many varieties of wild and specialty mushrooms are available today in supermarkets. This easy-to-assemble mushroom dish, adapted from a recipe from Dublin's Four Seasons Hotel (Simmonscourt Road), is perfect for vegetarians.

1 tablespoon canola oil	1 large egg
1 pound mixed mushrooms, coarsely chopped	½ cup half-and-half
1 tablespoon minced shallot	15 mini phyllo shells (see Note)
1 tablespoon white truffle oil	Fresh Parmesan shavings for garnish
1 tablespoon minced fresh flat-leaf parsley	Fresh chervil sprigs for garnish

Preheat the oven to 350°F.

In a large skillet over medium heat, heat the oil. Add the mushrooms and shallot and cook for 3 to 4 minutes, or until the mushrooms are soft but not browned. Stir in the truffle oil and parsley. Remove from the heat. In a small bowl, whisk together the egg and half-and-half. Stir it into the mushroom mixture.

Arrange the shells on a baking sheet. Divide the mushroom mixture among the shells and bake for 12 to 15 minutes, or until the filling is set. Remove from the oven. With a vegetable peeler, shave some Parmesan cheese on top of each tartlet and garnish with a sprig of chervil. Serve hot.

MAKES 15 TARTLETS

NOTE Look for Athens brand mini phyllo (or fillo) shells frozen in 15-shell boxes (see Resources, page 172).

Glamorgan Sausages

Glamorgan sausages are a traditional Welsh specialty. Perfect as a savory addition to high tea, these "sausages" are actually made of grated cheese and chopped leeks, which are bound together with bread crumbs and egg, then breaded and fried. Originally made with Glamorgan cheese, most recipes now suggest Caerphilly or a salty Cheddar cheese. In addition to being served with tea, Glamorgan sausages (*Selsig Morgannwg* in Welsh) can also be eaten hot for breakfast or cold for a picnic.

¾ cup fresh plain bread crumbs	Freshly ground pepper
4 ounces Caerphilly or Cheddar cheese, grated	1 large egg; plus 1 egg, separated
1 small leek, white and pale green parts, washed and diced	About ¼ cup milk
	All-purpose flour for coating
1 tablespoon minced fresh flat-leaf parsley	2 tablespoons canola oil
Pinch of dried mustard powder	2 tablespoons butter

In a large mixing bowl, combine the bread crumbs, cheese, leek, parsley, mustard, and a few grinds of pepper. Add 1 whole egg and 1 egg yolk and mix thoroughly. Add enough of the milk to bind the mixture together. Divide the mixture into 8 parts and shape into sausages.

Beat the remaining egg white until frothy. Dip the sausages in the egg white, then roll in the flour to coat.

In a large skillet over medium heat, heat 1 tablespoon each butter and oil. Add the sausages, a few at a time, and cook, turning frequently, for 5 to 8 minutes, or until golden brown. Repeat with the remaining oil, butter, and sausages. Serve hot or cold.

MAKES 8 SAUSAGES

Poached Lobster with Mini Molten Cheese Soufflés

London's Berkeley Hotel (Wilton Place, Knightsbridge) is an icon of style and service. Its famous drinking spot, the Blue Bar, has been a talking point of glossy magazines and gossip columns around the globe, and its chocolate-toned Caramel Room is home to a fashionable afternoon tea called Prêt-à-Portea (see page 63). Traditionalists will also enjoy this savory lobster dish—a bit like cheese fondue—where bite-size pieces of poached lobster (you may substitute shrimp) are dipped into a soufflé-like molten cheese with slightly crisp top.

Two 6-ounce fresh or frozen rock lobster tails or 8 large shrimp

2 tablespoons all-purpose flour

2 tablespoons unsalted butter, at room temperature

¾ cup milk

2 medium eggs, separated

2 tablespoons grated Cheddar cheese

1 teaspoon sea salt

Pinch of ground white pepper

Pinch of cayenne pepper

If the lobster is fresh, bring a medium saucepan of salted water to a boil. Add the tails, bring to a boil again, and cook for 5 to 6 minutes. Cook frozen lobster tails for 7 to 9 minutes. Remove from the heat and rinse under cold water. With kitchen shears or a large sharp knife, cut each tail in half lengthwise through the center. Discard the shells. If using shrimp, cook for 3 minutes, then rinse under cold water, peel, and devein. Cut the lobster into bite-size pieces and thread onto 4 wooden skewers or thread 2 shrimp onto each of 4 skewers. Alternately ask your fishmonger to poach the lobster or shrimp for you.

continued

Preheat the oven to 350°F.

In a small bowl, whisk together the flour and butter until smooth. In a small saucepan over medium heat, gently bring the milk to a boil. Add the butter mixture to the milk and whisk until smooth. Remove from the heat and let cool for 5 to 10 minutes. Beat in the egg yolks, cheese, salt, and white and cayenne peppers.

In a small bowl, beat the egg whites with an electric mixer until stiff peaks form. Fold the whites into the cheese mixture. Spoon the mixture into four 6-ounce ramekins and bake for 18 to 20 minutes, or until slightly risen. Remove from the oven and serve immediately with the poached lobster or shrimp.

SERVES 4

Crumpets, Scones & Fruit Breads

Egg coddlers are "finds" at Portobello Market, the antiques and collectibles fair that takes place every Saturday on Portobello Road in London's Notting Hill.

Another novelty is the tea party,
an extraordinary meal in that, being offered
to persons that have already dined well,
it supposes neither appetite nor thirst,
and has no object but distraction,
no basis but delicate enjoyment.

BRILLAT-SAVARIN, FRENCH EPICURE AND GASTRONOME

The second course in a proper afternoon tea is a selection of crumpets, scones, and fruit breads. The crumpets are served with butter and the scones with clotted or Devonshire cream—a thickened cream that you can make yourself (page 60) or buy at specialty food markets— raspberry or strawberry preserves (page 62), and often lemon curd (see page 125).

Fruit breads are offered along with the crumpets and scones. Not overly sweet, they are, according to the late Irish cookery writer Theodora Fitzgibbon, "a reminder of one's Celtic heritage." She says, "All the Celtic countries—Scotland, Ireland, Wales, even Brittany—have many things in common, including a similarity of language, cultural heritage, and a surprising number of foods general to all. There is little to choose between the Barm Brack of Ireland, the Bara Brith of Wales, and the Selkirk Bannock of Scotland." Despite what they're called, many of the breads begin with a lengthy soaking of dried fruits in tea and are a universal addition to this second course.

A Devon cream tea, or simply a cream tea, as its known in England's western counties of Devon, Cornwall, and Somerset, is a bit of a less formal affair and consists only of tea and scones, clotted cream, and fruit preserves. This simplified version, however, comes with some controversy.

If you use the Devonshire method, you would first split the scone in two horizontally, then cover each half with a helping of clotted cream and top with a teaspoon of jam. If you want your scone the Cornish way, first butter the scone, then spread it with a layer of jam and top it with a large spoonful of clotted cream. In Somerset, folks generally use the Devonshire method because Somerset borders Devon and not Cornwall. When scones are presented at tea, the hostess can suggest either method, and the controversy often adds to the enjoyment.

The Bramah Museum chronicles the history of both tea and coffee in London and the world.

THE BRAMAH MUSEUM of Tea and Coffee is a delightful tearoom and museum at 40 Southwark Street, near London Bridge. Founded by tea and coffee aficionado Edward Bramah, it's the world's first museum devoted entirely to the history of two of the world's most important commodities and chronicles their 400-year-old commercial and social history since arriving in Europe from the Far East and Africa.

Since the British played a major role in both the China trade and the development of production in India, Ceylon, and Africa, the museum tells the story from a British perspective. Through a series of ceramics, metalware, prints, and mechanical displays, one half of the museum covers all aspects of tea history. The second half of the museum is dedicated to coffee, showing how it spread around the world and how it is roasted and brewed. Seminars are offered periodically.

Crumpets

Located in the heart of London's Mayfair district, the Chesterfield (35 Charles Street) was once the home of the Earl of Chesterfield. The hotel still retains the charm and character of a bygone era and in its airy Conservatory, guests can choose from four distinctive afternoon teas—Devonshire, Champagne, Traditional, or Chocolate. Crumpets (adapted here) and scones follow the sandwich course and are served warm with lots of butter and jam or preserves.

½ cup water, heated to 110°F	½ teaspoon baking soda
2 teaspoons sugar	1½ cups milk, warmed
1 envelope active dry yeast	Butter, at room temperature
2½ cups all-purpose flour	Strawberry or raspberry jam for serving
1 teaspoon salt	

In a large bowl, combine the water, sugar, and yeast. Let the mixture sit for about 5 minutes, or until foamy. Stir in the flour, salt, baking soda, and milk. Cover and leave in a warm place for about 30 minutes, or until the mixture has risen.

Butter a large nonstick skillet and place it over low heat. Generously butter crumpet rings (see Resources page 171) or 2½-inch biscuit cutters. Place the rings in the skillet and fill each halfway with batter. Cook over low heat for 10 minutes, or until small holes appear and the top has started to dry. Remove the rings, turn the crumpets over, and cook for 1 to 2 minutes, or until lightly browned. Repeat with the remaining batter. Serve warm or toasted with butter and jam.

MAKES ABOUT 12 CRUMPETS

Scotch Pancakes

Scotch pancakes, also known as drop scones, are typically served in Scotland at tea-time rather than at breakfast. About the size of what Americans call "silver dollar pancakes," the recipes vary, so you might find some made with grated apples or spices. At the Caledonian Hotel (Princes Street), afternoon tea is served in the Castle Suite Lounge within view of Edinburgh Castle, and these tasty pancakes are always included. Like the Balmoral Hotel at the other end of the city's main thoroughfare, the "Caley," as locals call it, was built by the Caledonian railway company.

2 tablespoons light corn syrup, heated	1¼ cups buttermilk
3½ cups self-rising flour	2 large eggs
5 tablespoons sugar	Butter, at room temperature
½ teaspoon salt	Strawberry or raspberry jam for serving

In a large mixing bowl, combine the corn syrup, flour, sugar, and salt. In a separate small bowl, whisk together the buttermilk and eggs. Add the milk mixture to the flour mixture and whisk to form a smooth batter.

Heat a griddle or large skillet over medium-high heat for 1 minute. Brush the pan with butter. For each pancake, drop 1 heaping tablespoon batter onto the griddle, spacing the pancakes 1 inch apart. Cook for about 3 minutes, or until bubbles start to form on the surface. Turn the pancakes over and cook for 2 minutes longer, or until golden on the bottom. Working in batches, repeat with the remaining batter (regreasing if necessary between batches). Transfer the pancakes to a plate and cover with a tea towel to keep warm while you continue cooking. Serve warm with butter and jam.

MAKES ABOUT 24 PANCAKES

Traditional Scones

Dating from 1897, the Park Hotel (Kenmare, County Kerry) is nestled peacefully in an idyllic setting overlooking Kenmare Bay in southwest Ireland. When weather cooperates, the Park serves tea and traditional scones like these on linen-covered tables in terraced gardens overlooking the mountains and bay.

2¾ cups self-rising flour

⅓ cup sugar

½ cup (1 stick) unsalted butter, cold and cut into small pieces, plus more at room temperature for serving

1 large egg, beaten

¾ cup buttermilk

¾ cup (3 ounces) raisins

Sugar crystals for sprinkling (see Resources, page 173)

Clotted Cream (page 60) for serving (optional)

Strawberry jam or Lemon Curd (see page 125) for serving

Preheat the oven to 425°F. Line a baking sheet with parchment paper.

Combine the flour and sugar in a food processor. Add the ½ cup butter and pulse 8 to 10 times, or until the mixture resembles coarse crumbs. Transfer to a large bowl, then stir in the egg and buttermilk with a wooden spoon until a soft dough begins to form.

Transfer the dough to a lightly floured surface, and with floured hands, knead in the raisins. Roll out or pat the dough into a ½-inch-thick round. With a 2½-inch biscuit cutter, cut into rounds. Reroll the scraps and cut out additional rounds. Transfer to the prepared baking sheet and sprinkle the tops with sugar crystals.

Bake the scones for 15 to 18 minutes, or until golden. Remove from the oven and let cool for 10 minutes. Serve warm with butter or clotted cream, if desired, and jam.

MAKES 12 TO 14 SCONES

Raisin-Apple Scones

Since its opening in 1854, Claridge's Hotel (Brook Street, Mayfair) has welcomed royalty—from Queen Victoria to the Kings of Greece, Norway, and Yugoslavia, who stayed for the duration of World War II. Chances are they had tea in the Foyer and enjoyed scones filled with raisins and grated apples (adapted here). While currants and raisins are the most traditional addition, dried cranberries or blueberries, candied ginger, or fresh berries can also be used (see the variations that follow).

3 cups self-rising flour	1 large egg, beaten
½ cup sugar	1 small green apple, peeled, cored, and grated
¾ cup (1½ sticks) unsalted butter, cold and cut into small pieces, plus more at room temperature for serving	⅓ cup raisins
	Sugar crystals for sprinkling (see Resources, page 173)
1 cup buttermilk	Clotted Cream (page 60) for serving (optional)

Preheat the oven to 350°F. Line a baking sheet with parchment paper.

Combine the flour and sugar in a food processor. Add the ¾ cup butter and pulse 8 to 10 times, or until the mixture resembles coarse crumbs. Transfer to a large bowl, then stir in the buttermilk and egg with a wooden spoon until a soft dough begins to form.

Transfer the dough to a lightly floured work surface, and with floured hands, knead in the apple and raisins. Divide the dough in half and form each half into a ball. Flatten each into a 1-inch-thick disk. Place on the prepared baking sheet, and with a serrated knife that has been

continued

dipped into flour, cut each disk into 6 wedges. Sprinkle the tops with sugar crystals. Alternately you can bake these in large (8) or mini (16) cast-iron scone pans (see Resources, page 172).

Bake the scones for 25 to 30 minutes, or until the tops are golden and a skewer inserted into one of the wedges comes out clean. Remove from the oven and let cool for 10 minutes. Serve warm with butter or clotted cream, if desired.

MAKES 12 SCONES

VARIATIONS

Wicklow Blueberry and Cranberry Scones

At the Ritz-Carlton Powerscourt, Powerscourt Estate (Enniskerry, County Wicklow), the chef makes scones using dried cranberries and local blueberries for afternoon tea in the Sugar Loaf Lounge. Substitute 3 tablespoons dried blueberries and 2 tablespoons dried cranberries for the apple and raisins. Proceed with the recipe as directed.

Raisin-Ginger Scones

Substitute ⅓ cup chopped crystallized (candied) ginger for the apple and add the grated zest of 1 lemon. Proceed with the recipe as directed.

Strawberry Scones

For springtime "Pink Tea," substitute 1 cup sliced strawberries for the apple and raisins. Proceed with the recipe as directed.

Chocolate Scones

Afternoon tea at Edinburgh's landmark Balmoral Hotel (1 Princes Street) comes with dishes infused with local flavor—sandwiches made with Scottish salmon and Angus beef, Dundee cake, Scotch pancakes, traditional and chocolate scones. Served in the Bollinger Bar at the Palm Court (it's the only hotel in Scotland to host a Bollinger Champagne Bar), tea at the Balmoral is a decadent way to spend an afternoon.

2½ cups self-rising flour	1¼ cups heavy whipping cream or buttermilk
½ cup unsweetened cocoa powder	1 large egg yolk
½ cup sugar	Whole milk for brushing tops
½ cup (1 stick) unsalted butter, cold and cut into small pieces	Clotted Cream (page 60) for serving

Preheat the oven to 425°F. Line a baking sheet with parchment paper.

In a large bowl, whisk together the flour, cocoa, and sugar. Cut in the butter with a pastry blender or mix with your fingers until the mixture resembles coarse crumbs. In a small bowl, whisk together the cream and egg yolk. Stir the cream mixture into the flour mixture to blend.

Transfer the dough to a lightly floured surface and with floured hands, knead gently to bring the dough together. Roll out or pat the dough into a ¾-inch-thick round. With a 2½-inch biscuit cutter, cut out rounds. Reroll the scraps and cut out additional rounds. Transfer to the prepared baking sheet and brush the tops lightly with milk.

Bake the scones for 16 to 18 minutes, or until puffed and dry around the edges. Remove from the oven and let cool for a few minutes. Serve warm with clotted cream.

MAKES 16 TO 18 SCONES

Clotted Creams

The area surrounding Devon, Cornwall, and Somerset in the southwest of England is known for its dairy products, thanks to a mild climate, rich pastures, and the type of cows they tend—mainly Jerseys and Guernseys whose milk is rich in butterfat. Traditionally made by gently simmering large vats of milk until a thick layer of cream can be skimmed off the top, clotted cream is the gem of the area's dairy industry. Authentic clotted cream has the consistency of soft butter with a 55 to 60 percent fat content. It is so thick it does not need whipping. Also known as Devonshire, Devon, or Cornish clotted cream, it is available in fine supermarkets and gourmet shops worldwide. It's usually sold in small glass jars and has a shelf life of several months. If you can't find the real thing, the following, as well as Crème Fraîche (see Note page 30), are fantastic substitutes.

Clotted Cream

2⅔ cups heavy whipping cream | 2 tablespoons unsalted butter

In a medium saucepan over medium-low heat, combine the cream and butter. With a wooden spoon, stir gently until the mixture begins to simmer. Do not let it boil. Continue stirring and simmering for 20 to 25 minutes, or until the mixture is reduced by half and starts to thicken. Remove from the heat, transfer to a shallow glass dish, and let cool completely. Cover and refrigerate for at least 24 hours, or until it is smooth and thick. (Can be stored in the refrigerator for 1 week.)

MAKES ABOUT 1 CUP

Mock Clotted Cream

1 cup heavy whipping cream | 1 to 2 tablespoons sugar
½ cup mascarpone cheese (see Note)

In a chilled bowl, combine the cream, mascarpone, and sugar. Whisk for several minutes, or until the mixture forms a thick, smooth cream. Refrigerate until ready to use.

MAKES ABOUT 1½ CUPS

NOTE Mascarpone is a buttery-rich double (sometimes triple) cream made from cow's milk. Soft and smooth, the ivory-colored cheese is similar in texture to clotted cream. It is available in the dairy section of most supermarkets.

Strawberry Preserves

There are several excellent brands of strawberry preserves on the market (Bonne Maman, Tiptree, Elsenham, St. Dalfour, Hero, to name a few imported ones) that are delicious for topping scones, but nothing beats a homemade batch. Fresh strawberries are available in most areas in late spring and even a few jars of homemade preserves can be enjoyed for months.

2¼ pounds strawberries, rinsed and hulled

2¼ cups sugar

½ cup fresh lemon juice

Sterilize four ½-pint jars and lids (see Note).

Put the strawberries and sugar in a large nonreactive saucepan and pour the lemon juice over them. Leave for 10 to 15 minutes. Turn the heat to medium-low and cook, stirring gently, for 5 to 6 minutes, or until the sugar has dissolved. Increase the heat to high and bring to a rapid boil. Reduce the heat slightly and continue to boil, stirring frequently, for 20 to 25 minutes, or until the mixture begins to thicken. Skim off any foam that develops.

Ladle the mixture into the prepared jars, filling to within ¼ inch of the top. Wipe the rims with a dampened cloth and seal with lids.

MAKES 4 HALF PINTS

NOTE To sterilize jars and lids, run them through the high heat or sanitize cycle of your dishwasher, or put them in a large pot of water, bring to a boil, and let the water boil for about 5 minutes. Turn the heat down to simmer and leave the jars and lids in it until ready to fill. Dry thoroughly just before filling.

In London it's clear that tea is no passing trend. During the '70s and '80s, when times and lifestyles changed dramatically, the popularity of formal afternoon tea waned. But there's been a revival in recent years, as people once again enjoy its elegance. Afternoon tea is the hot new invitation, and everybody is getting in on the act.

Teapots and tea sets are hugely popular with London's style savvy inhabitants, and new shapes and concepts by design gurus such as Terence Conran, Zandra Rhodes, and Paul Smith are changing the way contemporary Londoners serve their daily cup. Even Wedgwood, renowned for its traditional bone china, has commissioned several up-and-coming young designers to produce a collection of cutting-edge tea services.

At the Berkeley Hotel (Wilton Place, Knightsbridge), Prêt-à-Portea is designed to add a creative twist to the classic elements of the traditional English afternoon tea. All the cakes and pastries are inspired by the latest fashion season's catwalk designs, such as Valentino chestnut crème handbags and Jimmy Choo's gold boot biscuits.

The pastry chef visits London fashion week shows to get his inspiration and then duplicates them as *pâtisserie* for the hotel's afternoon tea service in the Caramel Room. Fashionista delectables such as Emmanuel Ungaro blackberry mousse are served alongside a chocolate biscuit shaped as a Manolo Blahnik high-heeled shoe. Chilled Laurent Perrier Champagne is served in colorful Baccarat crystal flutes.

In Paris, too, where tea is also extremely popular (see The French Art of Tea), some hotels host "fashion teas," a combination of afternoon tea and haute couture. At Hotel Le Bristol (Rue du Faubourg Saint-Honoré) guests can enjoy an afternoon previewing the latest collections from famous Parisian fashion houses—Ungaro, Chapel, La Perla, and Jean-Louis Scherrer, to name a few—along with a tea service that includes fifteen teas served with scones and pastries created especially for each show.

Apricot-Walnut Loaf

Visitors to the Tea Room at Dublin's trendy Clarence Hotel (6–8 Wellington Quay), owned by Bono and The Edge of the Irish rock group U2, are often served this home-spun fruit loaf (adapted here) at afternoon tea.

3 cups (12 ounces) chopped dried apricots	1 teaspoon baking soda
1½ cups boiling water	¼ teaspoon grated nutmeg
2 tablespoons butter	¼ teaspoon ground cinnamon
1 cup muscovado sugar (see Resources, page 172)	½ cup raisins
	½ cup chopped walnuts
1 teaspoon salt	1 large egg, beaten
1½ cups all-purpose flour	2 tablespoons honey
1 cup whole-wheat flour	

Preheat the oven to 375°F. Butter a 9-by-5-by-3-inch loaf pan.

In a large bowl, combine the apricots, water, butter, sugar, and salt. Let sit for 10 minutes, or until the butter is melted. Into a separate bowl, sift together both flours, the baking soda, nutmeg, and cinnamon. Stir into the apricot mixture. Stir in the raisins, walnuts, and egg.

Transfer the batter to the prepared pan and bake for 60 to 65 minutes, or until the top is golden and a skewer inserted into the center comes out clean. Remove from the oven and let cool in the pan for 5 minutes on a wire rack. Invert the cake onto the rack and then turn it upright.

Meanwhile heat the honey in a microwave oven for 20 to 25 seconds, or until runny. Brush the honey over the top of the warm cake. Let cool completely before cutting into slices.

SERVES 8 TO 10

Banana Bread

The Merrion (Upper Merrion Street) is one of Dublin's most luxurious hotels. It was originally built for wealthy Irish merchants as four Georgian townhouses in the 1760s. In 1997, the listed buildings opened as a hotel. Chef Ed Cooney oversees the menu for afternoon tea, a genuine "event" for residents and visitors alike. One of his favorite tea offerings is this rich, dark banana bread that he glazes with warm apricot jam.

2 large ripe bananas, mashed	¾ cup milk
1¼ cups sugar	1¼ cups all-purpose flour
Pinch of salt	½ cup canola oil
3 large eggs, beaten	2 to 3 tablespoons apricot jam for glazing
2 teaspoons baking soda	

Preheat the oven to 325°F. Butter a 9-by-5-by-3-inch loaf pan.

In a large bowl, beat the bananas and sugar with an electric mixer on low speed for 4 to 5 minutes, or until smooth. Slowly beat in the salt and eggs.

In a small bowl, whisk together the baking soda and milk and slowly beat it into the banana mixture. Beat in the flour, and when incorporated, beat in the oil.

Transfer the batter to the prepared pan and bake for 60 to 65 minutes, or until the top is golden and a skewer inserted into the center comes out clean. Remove from the oven and let cool in the pan for 10 minutes on a wire rack. Run a knife around the edge of the pan, invert the bread onto the rack, and then turn it upright.

Meanwhile, heat the apricot jam in a microwave oven for 20 to 25 seconds, or until runny. Brush the jam over the top of the warm cake. Let cool completely before cutting into slices.

SERVES 8 TO 10

Tea Brack

At the Quay House (Clifden, County Galway), Julia Foyle serves an informal afternoon tea that always includes this loaf made with tea-soaked fruit.

4 cups (1 pound) mixed dried fruit, such as sultanas, dates, apricots, and cranberries, chopped

¼ cup candied orange peel

¼ cup chopped walnuts

¼ cup chopped pecans

1 teaspoon ground ginger

1 teaspoon pumpkin pie spice or Mixed Spice (see Note, page 76)

1¼ cups cold tea, such as Bewley's Irish Afternoon Tea (see Tea Note)

Butter, at room temperature

1 large egg, beaten

1 cup (packed) light brown sugar

2 cups self-rising flour

In a large bowl, combine the dried fruit, orange peel, walnuts, pecans, ginger, pumpkin pie spice, and tea. Let stand for 3 hours, or until the tea is absorbed.

Preheat the oven to 350°F. Butter a 9-by-5-by-3-inch loaf pan.

Stir the egg, sugar, and flour into the fruit mixture and mix until well combined. Transfer the batter to the prepared pan and bake for 65 to 70 minutes, or until the top is golden and a skewer inserted into the center comes out clean. Remove from the oven and let cool in the pan for 10 minutes on a wire rack. Invert the loaf onto the rack and then turn it upright. Let cool completely before cutting into slices. Serve with butter.

SERVES 10 TO 12

TEA NOTE Bewley's of Ireland is one of that country's most popular brands. Its Irish Afternoon Tea is a blend of African and Indian teas. Other popular Irish brands are Barry's and Lyons.

Spicy Marmalade Loaf

Marmalade was "invented" in 1797 in Dundee, Scotland, when James Keiller bought a cargo of bitter oranges and apples that were threatening to spoil after a Spanish ship sought shelter in the harbor during a storm. The thrifty Scotsman's wife turned the fruit into delicious pots of jams, the first batch of Keiller's original Dundee orange marmalade. Now popular throughout the world, it's also used in this teacake served at the Tea Room of Ballindalloch Castle, Banffshire, Scotland.

1 cup sugar	2 cups self-rising flour
1 cup milk	½ teaspoon baking soda
½ cup raisins or sultanas (golden raisins)	1 teaspoon pumpkin pie spice or Mixed Spice (see Note, page 76)
½ cup Keiller's Dundee orange marmalade or similar brand	
	Pinch of salt
½ cup (1 stick) unsalted butter	1 large egg, beaten

In a medium saucepan over medium heat, bring the sugar, milk, raisins, marmalade, and butter to a boil. Stir well, then remove from the heat and let cool completely.

Preheat the oven to 350°F. Line a 9-by-5-by-3-inch loaf pan with wax paper and spray with butter-flavored cooking oil spray.

With a wooden spoon, stir the flour, baking soda, pumpkin pie spice, salt, and egg into the marmalade mixture.

Transfer the batter to the prepared pan and bake for 60 minutes, or until the top is golden and a skewer inserted into the center comes out clean. Remove from the oven and let cool in the pan on a wire rack for 10 minutes. Invert the cake onto the rack and then turn it upright. Let cool completely before cutting into slices.

SERVES 8

Bara Brith

The Lake County House Hotel in the mid-Wales town of Llangammarch Wells, Powys, describes itself as an "architectural bagatelle." The half-timbered mock Tudor, built in 1840 as a hunting and fishing lodge and remodeled in the early 1900s, features verandas and French windows that give it a colonial air. It takes its name from a three-acre lake set in the middle of the property, which provides excellent salmon and trout fishing. The chef makes use of local ingredients and delights in serving traditional national specialties for afternoon tea like this yeasty Bara Brith, which translates to "speckled bread" in Welsh.

1 cup (4 ounces) currants	2¼ teaspoons active dry yeast
½ cup (2 ounces) sultanas (golden raisins)	¾ cup warm water
1 cup strong hot tea, such as Murroughs Welsh blend (see Tea Note)	2 tablespoons sugar
2½ cups all-purpose flour	1 large egg
1 teaspoon salt	2 tablespoons mixed candied peels
1 teaspoon pumpkin pie spice or Mixed Spice (see Note, page 76)	Butter, at room temperature
4 tablespoons vegetable shortening, such as Crisco	Honey for serving

In a large bowl, combine the currants, sultanas, and tea. Let sit for 2 to 3 hours, or until most of the tea is absorbed. Drain the fruit and discard the tea.

Combine the flour, salt, and pumpkin pie spice in a food processor fitted with a dough blade. Add the shortening and pulse 5 to 10 times, or until the mixture resembles coarse crumbs. In a medium bowl, whisk together the yeast, water, sugar, and egg. Add the yeast mixture to the flour mixture and process for 20 to 30 seconds, or until a dough forms. Dust a work surface with flour and turn out the dough.

With floured hands, work the currants, raisins, and candied peels into the dough. Form the dough into a ball and put it in an oiled bowl. Cover with a damp cloth and let rise in a warm place for about 1 hour, or until doubled in size.

Butter two 9-by-5-by-3-inch metal loaf pans. Return the dough to the work surface, punch it down to knock the air out, and divide it in half. Shape each half into a loaf and put them in the prepared pans. Let them rise again in a warm place for about 1 hour, or until doubled in size.

Preheat the oven to 375°F.

Bake for 20 to 22 minutes, or until golden. Remove the loaves from the oven and let them cool in the pans for about 15 minutes on a wire rack. Cut into slices and serve with butter and honey.

SERVES 8 TO 10

TEA NOTE Murroughs Welsh Brew (*Paned Gymreig* in Welsh) is a traditional blend of African and Indian teas selected for their strength, color, and smooth flavor.

Cup of Tea Cake

For such an opulent and elegant space as the Palm Court at London's Ritz Hotel (150 Piccadilly), this classic fruitcake is simply called "Cup of Tea Cake." Like other fruitcakes served at both afternoon and high tea (see page 31 for the difference), the fruit plumps up in a saucepan of hot, strong tea before being combined with the other ingredients. Lapsang Souchong gives this cake a strong, smoky flavor.

½ cup (1 stick) unsalted butter, plus more for greasing

1 cup strong black tea, such as Lapsang Souchong (see Tea Note)

2 cups (8 ounces) mixed dried fruit, such as raisins, sultanas, currants, dates, apricots, chopped

2 cups self-rising flour

1 teaspoon pumpkin pie spice or Mixed Spice (see Note, page 76)

1 teaspoon baking soda

1 cup sugar

1 large egg, beaten

In a small saucepan over medium heat, combine the ½ cup butter, tea, and fruit. Bring to a boil, then reduce the heat and simmer for 2 to 3 minutes. Remove from the heat and let the mixture cool completely.

Preheat the oven to 350°F. Butter a 9-by-5-by-3-inch loaf pan.

Into a large bowl, sift together the flour, pumpkin pie spice, and baking soda. Stir in the sugar, fruit mixture, and egg.

Transfer the batter to the prepared pan and bake for 45 to 50 minutes, or until the top is golden and a skewer inserted into the center comes out clean. Remove from the oven and let cool in the pan for 5 minutes on a wire rack. Invert the cake onto the rack and then turn it upright. Let cool completely before cutting into slices. Serve with butter.

SERVES 10 TO 12

TEA NOTE Lapsang Souchong tea comes from China's Fujian Province and Taiwan. Spreading the leaves out on bamboo trays and allowing smoke from pinewood to permeate the leaves gives this tea its flavor. Twinings calls its Lapsang Souchong "an adventurous tea with a unique smoked flavor and dark rich color."

Teatime Fruitcake

One of Ireland's finest hotels, Dromoland Castle (Newmarket-on-Fergus) is among the few that can trace its ownership back through history to Irish families of royal heritage. The castle offers guests fabulous accommodations and dining along with the experience of living like "landed gentry" amid the breathtaking scenery of County Clare. Enjoying afternoon tea is an integral part of the castle experience, and it's the perfect way to unwind after golfing, fishing, or riding on the castle's vast estate. Try this fruitcake at home for a reminder of Irish teatime, but be sure to start it at least two days before you want to serve it to let the fruit soak and the flavors meld.

1 cup water

1 cup (4 ounces) raisins

1 cup (4 ounces) sultanas (golden raisins)

2 ounces red glacé cherries

1½ tablespoons dark rum

1½ tablespoons sherry

1 teaspoon vanilla extract

½ cup (1 stick) unsalted butter, at room temperature, plus more for greasing

½ cup superfine sugar

2 large eggs

1 cup self-rising flour

1 teaspoon pumpkin pie spice or Mixed Spice (see Note)

The day before baking, in a medium saucepan over medium heat, bring the water to a boil. Stir in the raisins, sultanas, and cherries, and cook for 3 minutes. Drain the fruit and transfer to a small bowl. Stir in the rum, sherry, and vanilla. Let cool for 30 minutes, then cover and let stand for 24 hours at room temperature.

continued

On the day of baking, preheat the oven to 300°F. Line a 9-by-5-by-3-inch loaf pan with wax paper and butter the paper.

Beat the ½ cup butter and the sugar with an electric mixer until light and fluffy. Beat in the eggs, one at a time, beating well after each addition. With a wooden spoon, fold in the flour and pumpkin pie spice. Stir in the reserved fruit mixture.

Transfer the batter to the prepared pan and bake for 65 to 70 minutes, or until a skewer inserted into the center comes out clean. Remove from the oven and let cool completely in the pan on a wire rack. Invert the cake onto the rack, peel off the wax paper, and wrap the cake in aluminum foil. Let sit overnight at room temperature before cutting into slices.

SERVES 8 TO 10

NOTE To make Mixed Spice, put 1 tablespoon coriander seeds, 1 crushed cinnamon stick, 1 teaspoon whole cloves, and 1 teaspoon allspice berries in a spice or coffee grinder. Process until finely ground. Add 1 tablespoon freshly grated nutmeg and 2 teaspoons ground ginger. Mix thoroughly, stirring by hand. Store in an airtight container.

Dundee Cake

The top of this classic Scottish fruitcake is traditionally covered with blanched whole almonds. Light as well as spongy, the cake, named for the town of Dundee where it originated at the end of the nineteenth century, is a classic addition to afternoon tea. In addition to other Scottish traditional breads, you'll find it served for tea on board the Royal Scotsman, a luxury train that journeys through Scotland on a variety of routes (see page 157).

Unsalted butter for greasing, plus ¾ cup (1½ sticks)

2¼ cups all-purpose flour

1 teaspoon baking powder

½ teaspoon salt

¾ cup sugar

3 large eggs

½ cup milk

1 cup (4 ounces) sultanas (golden raisins)

½ cup currants

¼ cup candied orange or lemon peel

¼ cup chopped almonds

2 tablespoons Scotch whisky

TOPPING

20 to 24 blanched almonds

2 tablespoons milk

1 tablespoon sugar

Preheat the oven to 325°F. Butter a 9-inch round cake pan, line the bottom with wax paper, and butter the paper.

continued

Into a large bowl, sift together the flour, baking powder, and salt. In a medium bowl, beat the ¾ cup butter and the sugar with an electric mixer on medium until light and fluffy. Add the eggs, one at a time, beating well after each addition. Add the flour mixture and milk alternately to the butter mixture, beating after each addition. Fold in the sultanas, currants, candied peel, chopped almonds, and whisky.

Transfer the batter to the prepared pan. Smooth the top with a damp spatula or with wet hands. Cover with aluminum foil or parchment paper and bake for 50 minutes.

Remove from the oven and remove the foil. Starting at the center, arrange the blanched almonds over the top in concentric circles. Return the cake to the oven and bake, uncovered, for 45 to 50 minutes longer, or until the top is golden and a skewer inserted into the center comes out clean. Remove from the oven.

Heat the milk with the sugar for 1 to 2 minutes, or until the sugar dissolves. Brush it over the cake to create a dry glaze. Let cool in the pan for 15 to 20 minutes on a wire rack. Invert the cake onto the rack and then turn it upright. Let cool completely before cutting into slices. (Can be stored in an airtight container for up to 2 weeks.)

SERVES 8 TO 10

Teatime Sweets

British designer Zandra Rhodes' signature butterflies and wiggle lines adorn her china collection made by Royal Doulton. London's Mandeville Hotel presents its afternoon designer teas on the china.

Love and scandal are the
best sweeteners of tea.

HENRY FIELDING, ENGLISH NOVELIST

THE THIRD AND FINAL COURSE in an afternoon tea service is, without question, the pièce de résistance of the menu. Sometimes simply called the "sweets" course, the selection of cookies, cakes, pastries, and tarts is anything but simple, with luxurious French pastries generally making an appearance alongside more traditional sweets like shortbreads, Swiss rolls, charlottes, cupcakes, meringues, and mousses.

The sweets course is where bakers and pastry chefs really get to show their stuff, and home cooks—with a few tricks to make you look like a pro—should have no fear of trying. With some kitchen "assistance" from prepared ingredients like frozen puff pastry and phyllo shells, piecrust dough, chocolate cups, and sweet tart shells, you'll enjoy preparing these teatime sweets as much as your guests will enjoy eating them.

Have you had cookies made with tea lately? If not, you'll enjoy a recipe for Lady Grey Cookies, delicious tea-infused creations from Twinings, London's 300-year-old tea company. If meringues have been absent from your baking repertoire, you'll love the recipe from Glasgow's world-famous Willow Tea Rooms, premises designed by legendary Scottish architect Charles Rennie Mackintosh in 1904. Intimidated by tarts? You'll be pleasantly surprised to see how simple it is to create Lemon Cream or Lemon Curd Tartlets, and how you can put "tempting tarts" on every afternoon tea menu with a collection of easy-as-pie shells and fillings.

To put the "wow" factor into your afternoon tea, you can dazzle your guests with Battenberg Cake—a distinctive pink-and-white checked cake covered in marzipan and the current darling of afternoon tea at Dublin's Westin Hotel—or with ethereal Chocolate Mille-Feuilles, like the ones served in the Palm Court at the Ritz London. For more down-to-earth baking, you can choose from two varieties of homey shortbread, Scotland's national teatime treasure, plain and simple cupcakes (also known as fairy cakes), or Victoria Sponge, a light, jam-filled layer cake named for the long-reigning English monarch.

Chocolate always plays a major role in the sweets course, from the Extreme Chocolate Biscuit Brownie served at Claridge's—it's actually a two layer concoction of nutty brownie and chocolate cream frosting—to the subtle-but-rich Earl Grey tea-infused Chocolate Mousse from London's Four Seasons Hotel or the Chocolate and Banana Charlottes served at the Savoy. An important tip for any chocolate recipe: the better the chocolate (70 percent or higher cocoa content), the richer the flavor.

For a fabulous finish to the sweets course, add a glass of Champagne—they offer Bollinger at the Balmoral, Tattinger at the Merrion, and Dom Pérignon at Claridge's—sit back, and wait for the raves to roll in.

The distinctive flavor of Twinings Earl Grey tea spices up sweets like chocolate mousse and butter cookies.

Shortbread

Regardless of where you travel in Scotland, you find shortbread served at afternoon tea. Queen Victoria, who found the plain and simple delicacies of the Scottish baking tradition much to her taste, was said to be very fond of this cookie, which you can make in a wide variety of shapes and in shortbread molds. This shortbread is served to visitors at Rothiemurchus Estate, located in the heart of the Cairngorms National Park, Aviemore, Inverness-shire.

Unsalted butter for greasing, plus 1 cup (2 sticks) at room temperature

½ cup superfine sugar, plus more for sprinkling

2 cups all-purpose flour

1 cup semolina flour (see Resources, page 172)

Preheat the oven to 300°F. Butter a 9-inch square baking pan.

In a medium bowl, beat the 1 cup butter and the sugar with an electric mixer on medium speed until smooth. Add the flours and mix to a smooth dough. Press the dough evenly over the bottom of the prepared pan. With a fork, pierce the dough all over. Bake for about 50 minutes, or until the shortbread is pale brown in the center and golden at the edges. Remove from the oven and sprinkle with additional sugar while still warm. Let cool in the pan before cutting into 24 pieces.

MAKES 2 DOZEN COOKIES

Pistachio, Lemon, and Vanilla Shortbread

According to Condé Nast *Traveller*, Kinloch Lodge (Isle of Skye, Scotland) is one of the world's top 100 small hotels. Here Lord and Lady Claire MacDonald—an award-winning cook and food writer who has revitalized traditions of highland hospitality—welcome guests throughout most of the year to their inn. A visitor wrote in its guest book, "Your welcome is as warm as the fires that burn in every grate," and Lady Claire's food is as good as any you'll find in Scotland. Here she updates a traditional shortbread recipe by adding lemons and pistachios.

Unsalted butter for greasing, plus 1 cup (2 sticks), cold and cut into small pieces

1½ cups all-purpose flour

½ cup sugar

½ cup semolina flour (see Resources, page 172)

1½ teaspoons grated lemon zest

1 teaspoon vanilla extract

1 cup (4 ounces) shelled natural pistachios, coarsely chopped

Preheat the oven to 325°F. Butter a 13-by-9-by-2-inch metal baking pan.

Put the all-purpose flour, sugar, and semolina in a food processor and process for 5 to 10 seconds. Add the 1 cup butter, lemon zest, and vanilla extract. Pulse 8 to 10 times, or until the mixture resembles coarse meal. Turn the dough out into a bowl. Add the nuts and knead gently to combine. Press the dough evenly over the bottom of the prepared pan. With a fork, pierce the dough all over.

Bake for 33 to 35 minutes, or until the shortbread is pale brown in the center and golden at the edges. Remove from the oven and cool in the pan on a wire rack for 10 minutes. Cut lengthwise into 6 strips, then cut each strip crosswise into 4 pieces. Cool completely in the pan.

MAKES 2 DOZEN COOKIES

SHORTBREAD, which is neither short nor bread, originated in Scotland as a byproduct of the country's abundant dairy industry. Throughout British culinary history, milk, cream, butter, and cheese have been common ingredients in baking. In ancient times butter was combined with oatmeal, another peasant staple, and baked into "short" cakes, so called because of the high butter content that made them very crumbly. In the sixteenth century, shortbread grew more refined as it became popular with Britain's expanding middle class and the first recipes for it were written.

In Scotland, each region has its own variations and tricks for achieving the perfect texture (many cooks even mix the dough by hand to ensure that it's not overhandled, which would cause heaviness). In some areas eggs, cream, spices, or other flavorings are added to the basic butter-flour-sugar recipe. The shape also varies from region to region. Some cooks like to pat the dough into a square pan and cut the shortbread into fingers; some prefer to cut it out into rounds; and others like to use a shortbread mold, which gives the tops their unique decoration.

Walkers, the oldest and most honored shortbread company in the world, has been making shortbread since 1898 in the Scottish highland town of Aberlour-on-Spey using original recipes from its founder Joseph Walker. Considered a true Scottish classic, Walkers shortbread comes in all shapes and sizes—round, mini, fingers, triangles, and petticoat tails—and in flavors ranging from plain and chocolate chip to stem ginger, almond, and hazelnut. Walkers has won more international awards for excellence than any other shortbread company.

One of the newest shortbread brands has Irish origins, from County Cork native Rachel Gaffney (see Resources, page 172). Her eponymous cookies, made in four flavors—traditional butter, lemon zest, coconut, and ground espresso with shaved chocolate—are delicious with a cup of tea.

Extreme Biscuit Brownie

Claridge's Hotel (Brook Street, Mayfair) garnered the U.K. Tea Guild's coveted "Top Afternoon Tea Award" in 2006 and an "Award of Excellence" in 2007 and 2008. The hotel offers tea in its luxurious art deco Foyer, which was restored in 1998 by architect-designer Thierry Despont to celebrate the hotel's centenary. The pastry chef there adds a third layer of chocolate to these brownies, but I think you'll be completely satisfied with only two.

BROWNIE BISCUITS	CHOCOLATE TOPPING
Cooking oil spray	⅓ cup half-and-half
4 ounces (4 squares) semisweet chocolate	½ cup (1 stick) unsalted butter, cut into small pieces
¾ cup (1½ sticks) unsalted butter	2 tablespoons sugar
2 cups sugar	8 ounces (8 squares) semisweet chocolate, cut into small pieces
3 large eggs	1 teaspoon vanilla extract
1 teaspoon vanilla extract	
1 cup all-purpose flour	
½ teaspoon baking powder	
Pinch of salt	
½ cup chopped walnuts	
¼ cup chopped pecans	

TO MAKE THE BROWNIES Preheat the oven to 350°F. Line an 8-inch square baking pan with aluminum foil long enough to extend over the sides of the pan. Spray the foil with cooking oil spray.

In a large microwave-safe bowl, combine the chocolate and butter. Microwave on high for 2 minutes, or until the butter is melted. With a wooden spoon, stir until the butter and chocolate are smooth. Stir in the sugar, then whisk in the eggs and vanilla. Add the flour, baking powder, salt, and nuts and mix well.

Transfer the batter to the prepared pan and bake for 30 to 35 minutes, or until a skewer inserted into the center comes out almost clean (center should still be slightly moist).

Remove from the oven and let cool in the pan on a wire rack for 10 minutes. Using the foil handles, lift the brownie cake out of the pan and return to the wire rack. Let cool for another 10 minutes.

TO MAKE THE TOPPING In a large heavy saucepan over medium heat, combine the half-and-half, butter, and sugar. Stir until blended. Add the chocolate and whisk until melted and smooth. Reduce the heat to medium-low and cook for 4 to 5 minutes, or until the mixture is thick, syrupy, and beginning to bubble. Remove from the heat and stir in the vanilla. Beat slowly with a wooden spoon for 5 to 10 minutes, or until the mixture thickens slightly. Pour the chocolate over the brownie cake and spread with an offset spatula. Refrigerate for 10 to 15 minutes, or until the topping is firm.

Cut the cake into four 2-inch-wide strips, then cut each strip in half.

MAKES 8 BROWNIES

Meringues

Glasgow's Willow Tea Rooms (217 Sauchiehall and 97 Buchanan Street) are the only tearooms where architect Charles Rennie Mackintosh had complete control over every aspect of the design (see page 92). The tearooms were named for the Scottish-Gaelic word *Sauchiehall*, which means "alley of the willows," and the willows theme is featured throughout the building. In 1995 the prestigious British Tea Council invited the Willow to become one of the founding members of the Guild of Tea Rooms. The Willow serves luscious pastries and cakes, including these meringues sandwiched with whipped cream.

| 4 large egg whites, at room temperature | 1 cup superfine sugar |

Preheat the oven to 300°F. Line 2 baking sheets with parchment paper.

In a large, dry bowl, beat the egg whites with an electric mixer on medium-low speed for 2 to 3 minutes, or until foamy. Increase the speed to medium-high and continue to beat until soft peaks form. Do not overbeat or the whites will collapse. (To test for the right consistency, tip the bowl at an angle; if the mixture doesn't slide out, it's ready to add the sugar.)

Gradually beat in the sugar (about 1 tablespoon at a time), beating well after each addition, and continue to beat until thick, glossy peaks are formed. Drop tablespoons of the mixture in mounds onto the prepared sheets (about 7 mounds per sheet), spacing them several inches apart.

Reduce the oven temperature to 275°F and bake for 60 minutes, or until lightly colored. Turn off the oven and leave the meringues in for 60 minutes longer. Remove from the oven and serve immediately, or store in an airtight container for up to a day.

MAKES 14 LARGE MERINGUES

CHARLES RENNIE MACKINTOSH was a turn-of-the-century Scottish architect, water-colorist, and designer in the Arts and Crafts movement. He was also the main exponent of art nouveau in Scotland. In 1896, Mackintosh met Catherine Cranston (widely known as Kate Cranston or simply Miss Cranston), an entrepreneurial local businesswoman and daughter of a Glasgow tea merchant. She was a strong believer in the temperance move-ment, which was becoming increasingly pop-ular in Glasgow at the time, and conceived the idea of a series of "art tearooms"—ven-ues where people could meet to relax and enjoy nonalcoholic refreshments in a variety of different "rooms" within the same build-ing. This proved to be the start of a long work-ing relationship between Miss Cranston and Mackintosh, and between 1896 and 1917 he designed and restyled interiors in all four of her Glasgow tearooms, often in collabora-tion with his wife, Margaret MacDonald.

In 1903, he was commissioned to com-pletely design the proposed new tearooms on Sauchiehall Street. The name "Sauchie-hall" is derived from *saugh*, the Scots word for a willow tree, and *haugh*, meaning meadow. This provided the starting point for Mackin-tosh's ideas for the design theme, and for the first time, he was given responsibility for not only the interior design and furniture but also for the full detail of the internal layout and exterior architectural treatment. These tearooms came to be known as the Willow Tea Rooms, and they are the best-known and most important work that Mackintosh undertook for Miss Cranston.

Willow was the basis for the name of the tearooms, but it also formed an integral part of the decorative motifs employed in the interior design and much of the timberwork used in the building fabric and furniture. Described at the time as "a fantasy for after-noon tea," the room was intimate and richly decorated in a gray, purple, and white color scheme, complemented by white tablecloths and blue willow-pattern crockery.

Following the death of her husband in 1917, Miss Cranston sold her businesses, and the Willow Tea Rooms saw many owners until eventually closing in the early 1980s. Glasgow businesswoman Anne Mulhern reopened the tearooms at 217 Sauchiehall Street in 1983 and refurbished them to re-create the original color scheme and furnishings. Immediately the Willow became an extremely popular destination for visitors to the city.

In July 1997, the Willow expanded beyond the original Sauchiehall Street site with the opening of the Willow Tea Rooms at 97 Buchanan Street. The tearooms are enormously popular today and are the most famous of the many Glasgow tearooms that opened in the late nineteenth and early twentieth centuries.

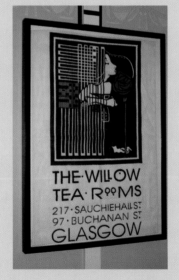

The Art Nouveau designs of Charles Rennie Mackintosh are used throughout Glasgow's Willow Tea Rooms.

Chocolate Mille-Feuille

Mille-Feuille (pronounced meel-FWEE) is French for "a thousand leaves." Also called napoleons, puff pastry layers are stacked and filled with *crème pâtissière* (a thick, flour-based pastry cream), jam, fruit, or whipped cream. They are generally topped with a thin icing or fondant. At the Ritz London (150 Piccadilly), the chef makes his own puff pastry and chocolate filling and then pipes lines of chocolate over the top. For equally delicious results, you can use frozen puff pastry and finish with a simple dusting of confectioners' sugar.

CRÈME PÂTISSIÈRE

3 large egg yolks

4 tablespoons superfine sugar

2½ tablespoons all-purpose flour

1 tablespoon unsweetened cocoa powder

1 cup plus 2 tablespoons milk

2 teaspoons vanilla extract

1 sheet frozen puff pastry (from a 17-ounce package), such as Pepperidge Farm brand

⅓ cup heavy whipping cream

Confectioners' sugar for dusting

Fresh berries for garnish

TO MAKE THE CRÈME PÂTISSIÈRE In a small bowl, beat the egg yolks and 1 tablespoon of the sugar with an electric mixer on medium speed until light and fluffy. Sift the flour and cocoa over the egg mixture and beat until fully incorporated.

In a small saucepan over medium heat, bring the milk to a boil with the remaining 3 tablespoons sugar and the vanilla. Once it boils, whisk a little of the hot milk mixture into the egg mixture, then stir the egg mixture back into the saucepan. Cook over medium heat, stirring constantly, for 3 to 4 minutes, or until the mixture boils and thickens. Remove from the heat, pour into a bowl, and place a piece of plastic wrap directly onto the surface of the custard to prevent a skin from forming. Cool completely, then refrigerate for 1 to 2 hours or overnight.

Preheat the oven to 400°F. Line a baking sheet with parchment paper.

Thaw the pastry at room temperature for 40 minutes. Unfold on a lightly floured surface. Cut into 3 strips along fold marks. Cut each strip into 4 rectangles and space them 2 inches apart on the prepared pan. Cover the pastry with a piece of parchment paper and put a second baking sheet on top to prevent the pastry from puffing up. Bake for 20 minutes, or until the pastry is golden. Remove from the oven, remove the baking sheet and paper, and transfer the pastry to a wire rack to cool.

Whip the heavy cream with an electric mixer until stiff peaks form. Stir the *crème pâtissière*, then fold in the whipped cream. Spread 4 pieces of pastry with 2 tablespoons each of the filling. Top with another layer of pastry, spread with 2 tablespoons of additional filling, and top with the remaining pastry layer. At serving time, sprinkle with confectioners' sugar and garnish with fresh berries.

MAKES 4 PASTRIES

Mille-Feuille with Roasted Fruits

The Shelbourne Hotel (27 St. Stephen's Green) has always been an integral part of Dublin's literary, social, artistic, and political traditions, including serving as the venue for the drafting of the Irish Constitution in 1922. If you go for tea in the Lord Mayor's Lounge, you might be offered this pastry (adapted here) from the sweets trolley.

Crème Pâtissière (page 94)	1 plum, pitted and sliced
1 sheet frozen puff pastry (from a 17-ounce package), such as Pepperidge Farm brand	½ pear, peeled, cored, and sliced
	½ Granny Smith apple, peeled, cored, and sliced
ROASTED FRUITS	2 tablespoons superfine sugar
¼ cup blueberries	3 tablespoons olive oil
¼ cup sliced strawberries	2 tablespoons honey
¼ cup sliced green grapes	Pinch each salt and pepper

Prepare the Crème Pâtissière (omitting the unsweetened cocoa powder) and bake the puff pastry as directed for Chocolate Mille-Feuille.

TO ROAST THE FRUITS Preheat the oven to 325°F. In a large bowl, combine the fruits, sugar, olive oil, honey, salt, and pepper. Transfer the mixture to a rimmed baking sheet and roast for 15 to 18 minutes, or until the fruits begin to release their juices. Turn once or twice to coat all the fruits with the released juices. Remove from the oven and let cool.

Assemble as directed on page 95 and top with the roasted fruit.

MAKES 4 PASTRIES

Earl Grey Chocolate Mousse

Earl Grey tea was named after Charles Grey, prime minister to King William IV. One legend suggests that when Grey went as part of a trade delegation to China in 1834, he saved the life of a mandarin's son who was drowning. As a thank-you gift, the grateful mandarin gave the diplomat a recipe for a blend of tea that Grey later passed on to his tea merchant to re-create for his private use. Generally served without milk or lemon, Earl Grey is actually a plain black tea infused with the citrus flavor of bergamot (similar to orange blossoms). This gives a bright, tart, and refreshing taste to the tea, perfectly suited as an infusion in this mousse from London's Four Seasons Hotel (Hamilton Place, Park Lane). The dessert is one of the most popular offerings on the afternoon tea menu, and the chef recommends brut Champagne such as Pol Roger Extra Dry White Foil to accompany it.

3 ounces dark chocolate, broken into pieces

3 ounces milk chocolate, broken into pieces

2 cups heavy whipping cream

3 Earl Grey tea bags

3 large eggs, separated

½ cup sugar

Put the dark and milk chocolates in a microwave-safe bowl and microwave on high for 2 minutes. Stir until smooth.

In a small saucepan over medium heat, combine 1 cup of the cream and the tea bags. Bring slowly to a boil, then remove from the heat. With a spoon, press firmly on the tea bags to extract maximum flavor. Remove and discard the tea bags. Pour the mixture over the chocolate and stir until smooth.

In a small bowl, whip the remaining 1 cup cream with an electric mixer on medium speed until stiff peaks form. In a large bowl, beat the egg yolks and sugar with an electric mixer until pale and thick. In a separate small bowl, beat the egg whites with an electric mixer on medium-high speed until stiff peaks form. Combine the egg yolk mixture with the chocolate mixture, then fold in the whipped cream and egg whites. Spoon the mixture into eight 4-ounce ramekins and refrigerate for 2 to 3 hours, or until semifirm. Serve with madeleines or shortbread, if you like.

SERVES 8

NOTE People who are pregnant, elderly, or with medical problems that have impaired their immune systems should avoid eating raw eggs.

Gooseberry Mousse

Llangoed Hall, a country house in southern Wales, is the brainchild of Sir Bernard Ashley, husband of the late designer Laura Ashley. Each room in this dignified Jacobean mansion is decorated with antiques and furnishings from Elanbach, Sir Bernard's textile and design company. The kitchen relies on local produce such as the gooseberries in this mousse, which helped the hotel recently win the U.K. Tea Guild's Award of Excellence.

3 large egg whites

¼ cup water

1½ cups sugar

1¾ cups gooseberries, such as Landsberg brand, drained, plus 10 for garnish (see Resources, page 171)

1 tablespoon granulated gelatin

1 cup heavy whipping cream

In a medium bowl, whip the egg whites with an electric mixer on high speed until soft peaks form.

In a small saucepan over medium heat, bring the water and ½ cup of the sugar to a boil. Boil until all the sugar dissolves. Gradually whisk the syrup into the egg whites until fully blended.

In another small saucepan over medium heat, combine the gooseberries and remaining 1 cup sugar. Cook for 5 to 6 minutes, or until the gooseberries begin to break up and the sugar dissolves. With an immersion blender, purée the gooseberries until smooth. Transfer the gooseberry purée to a medium bowl and sprinkle the gelatin over it. Let cool for 5 minutes.

In a small bowl, whip the cream with an electric mixer until soft peaks form. Fold the whipped cream and egg whites into the gooseberries. Spoon the mousse into ten 3-ounce glasses and put a gooseberry on top of each. Refrigerate for 2 to 3 hours, or until set.

SERVES 10

Chocolate-Orange Tea Cake

The Athenaeum (116 Piccadilly) is located in the heart of London across from Green Park. It offers lovely accommodations and delicious afternoon teas "to revitalize and reward in an essentially English way." Traditional classics from the cake stall include Granny's teacakes, like this dark chocolate and orange cake that takes on a whole new dimension when accompanied by a glass of Champagne.

2 cups self-rising flour	Grated zest of 1 orange
2 tablespoons unsweetened cocoa powder	1 cup (2 sticks) unsalted butter, at room temperature
½ cup sweetened chocolate powder, such as for chocolate milk	
½ cup milk	1 cup sugar
2 tablespoons orange marmalade	4 large eggs

Preheat the oven to 325°F. Spray a 10-inch bundt pan with cooking spray with flour.

Into a large bowl, sift together the flour, cocoa powder, and chocolate powder. Set aside. In a small bowl, whisk together the milk, marmalade, and orange zest. Set aside.

In a separate bowl, beat the butter and sugar with an electric mixer on medium speed until light and fluffy.

Add the eggs, one at a time, beating well after each addition. Fold in the flour mixture, then stir in the marmalade mixture.

Transfer the batter to the prepared pan and bake for 45 to 50 minutes, or until a skewer inserted into the center comes out clean. Remove from the oven and let cool 10 minutes in the pan. Invert onto a wire rack and let cool completely before cutting into slices.

SERVES 10 TO 12

Chocolate and Banana Charlottes

At London's Savoy Hotel (Strand), the chef makes these charlottes for the sweets course. To intensify the chocolate experience at the Savoy, the chef makes homemade chocolate ladyfingers and fills the mold with chocolate mousse and lime-soaked bananas. Home cooks might like this adapted recipe that substitutes chocolate sponge cake for the ladyfingers and uses it to line ramekins for individual charlottes.

MARINATED BANANAS

1 large banana, sliced

Grated zest and juice of 1 lime

¼ cup Simple Syrup (see Note)

CHOCOLATE MOUSSE

3 ounces (3 squares) semisweet chocolate, broken into pieces

½ cup heavy whipping cream

1 large egg white

2 tablespoons sugar

CHOCOLATE SPONGE CAKE

6 ounces (6 squares) semisweet chocolate, broken into pieces

5 large eggs, separated

¾ cup plus 2 tablespoons granulated sugar

Confectioners' sugar for dusting

TO MARINATE THE BANANAS Put the banana slices in a small bowl and sprinkle the lime zest and pour the juice and simple syrup over them. Cover and refrigerate for 1 hour.

TO MAKE THE MOUSSE Put the chocolate in a microwave-safe bowl and microwave on high for 2 minutes. Stir until smooth.

In a small bowl, whip the cream with an electric mixer on medium until soft peaks form. In another small bowl, beat the egg white with an electric mixer on medium speed, gradually

continued

adding the sugar, and continue to beat until soft peaks form. Gradually fold the egg white into the chocolate, then fold in the whipped cream. Cover and refrigerate for at least 1 hour and up to 24 hours.

TO MAKE THE CAKE Preheat the oven to 350°F. Line a 15-by-10-inch jelly-roll pan with wax paper. Spray the wax paper with cooking oil spray. Put the chocolate in a microwave-safe bowl and microwave on high for 2 minutes. Stir until smooth. Let cool for about 10 minutes.

In a large bowl, beat the egg yolks and granulated sugar with an electric mixer on medium speed until light and fluffy. Gradually whisk in the melted chocolate. In a medium bowl, beat the egg whites with an electric mixer on medium speed until stiff peaks form. Slowly fold one quarter of the whites into the chocolate mixture to loosen it, then gently fold in the rest. Pour into the prepared pan and spread evenly to the corners. Bake for 15 to 20 minutes, or until the cake rises and is firm. Remove from the oven and invert onto a large sheet of wax paper to cool.

With a 3-inch biscuit cutter, cut 8 rounds out of the cake, cutting them close together. Cut the remaining cake into four 8-by-1-inch strips, then cut each strip crosswise in half. Put a cake round in the bottom of each of four 4-ounce ramekins and line the sides with the cake strips. Divide the reserved mousse among the ramekins, top with the bananas (reserving any liquid), then top with the remaining cake round. Press down gently. Cover and refrigerate for 2 to 3 hours, or until firm.

Run a knife around the sides of the ramekins and invert onto serving plates. Spoon any remaining banana marinade over the top and dust with confectioners' sugar.

SERVES 4

NOTE To make Simple Syrup, combine 3 parts water to 1 part sugar. Cook over low heat until the mixture is clear, then boil for 1 to 2 minutes. Let cool. Refrigerate the unused portion.

Chocolate-Orange Gâteau

The combination of chocolate and orange is a popular one, and at Adare Manor Hotel and Golf Resort (Adare, County Limerick), the chef kicks up the intensity of the two by filling a sponge cake with chocolate-orange mousse and finishing it with a chocolate glaze. The Drawing Room of the eighteenth-century manor is the perfect spot for afternoon tea.

CHOCOLATE-ORANGE MOUSSE

5 ounces (5 squares) dark chocolate

1 cup heavy whipping cream

2 large egg whites

1 tablespoon Cointreau or similar orange liqueur

2 tablespoons finely grated orange zest

CAKE

¾ cup all-purpose flour

1 teaspoon baking powder

¼ teaspoon salt

3 large eggs

1 cup granulated sugar

⅓ cup water

¼ cup ground almonds

Confectioners' sugar for dusting

CHOCOLATE GLAZE

¼ cup heavy whipping cream

⅓ cup water

⅓ cup sugar

2 tablespoons unsweetened cocoa powder

2 teaspoons granulated gelatin

continued

TO MAKE THE MOUSSE Put the chocolate in a microwave-safe bowl and microwave on high for 2 minutes. Stir until smooth. In a small bowl, whip the cream with an electric mixer on medium until soft peaks form. In another small bowl, beat the egg whites with an electric mixer on medium speed until soft peaks form. Gradually fold the egg whites into the chocolate, then fold in the whipped cream. Stir in the Cointreau and orange zest. Cover and refrigerate for at least 1 hour and up to 24 hours.

TO MAKE THE CAKE Preheat the oven to 375°F. Line a 15-by-10-inch jelly-roll pan with wax paper. Spray the wax paper with cooking oil spray. Also line a 9-by-5-by-3-inch loaf pan with aluminum foil long enough to extend over the long sides of the pan.

Into a small bowl, sift together the flour, baking powder, and salt. In a large bowl, beat the eggs and granulated sugar with an electric mixer on medium speed for about 5 minutes, or until thick and lemon colored. Beat in the water on medium speed, then stir in the flour mixture and ground almonds. Transfer the batter to the prepared jelly-roll pan and smooth the top with a spatula, spreading the batter to the corners.

Bake the cake for 15 to 17 minutes, or until golden and the center springs back when lightly touched. Remove from the oven and invert the pan onto a clean kitchen towel that has been dusted with confectioners' sugar. Let cool for about 10 minutes. Gently peel off the wax paper and cut the cake into three 8-by-4-inch rectangles.

TO MAKE THE GLAZE In a small saucepan over medium heat, bring the cream, water, and sugar to a boil. Whisk in the cocoa and gelatin. Place the pan over a large bowl filled with ice and let cool, stirring once or twice, for 10 to 15 minutes, or until the mixture begins to set.

Place one cake rectangle in the bottom of the prepared loaf pan, then spread half of the mousse on top. Repeat with another cake rectangle and the remaining mousse, then cover with the final layer of cake. Spread the chocolate glaze over the top and refrigerate for 1 to 2 hours, or until completely set.

Using the foil handles, lift the cake out of the pan. Place it on a flat surface, peel the foil away from the sides, and cut the cake into slices.

SERVES 8

Gingerbread and Treacle Cake

Molasses, called "dark treacle" in the U.K. and Ireland, is a popular flavoring in ginger-bread and adds both taste and color to it. Upon arrival at the Howard, a Georgian-style boutique hotel in the center of Edinburgh (34 Great King Street), guests are treated to tea and gingerbread (adapted here). Serve it with whipped cream or a dollop of crème fraîche and dust with confectioners' sugar.

2 cups all-purpose flour

1 teaspoon baking soda

1¾ teaspoons ground ginger

1¼ teaspoons ground cinnamon

1 teaspoon pumpkin pie spice or Mixed Spice (see Note, page 76)

Pinch of salt

⅔ cup dark molasses

1 cup milk

½ cup (1 stick) unsalted butter, at room temperature

½ cup (packed) dark brown sugar

2 large eggs, beaten

Confectioners' sugar for dusting

Whipped cream or Crème Fraîche (see Note, page 30) for serving

Preheat the oven to 325°F. Spray a 9-inch square or round baking pan with cooking oil. Dust with flour.

Into a large bowl, sift together the flour, baking soda, ginger, cinnamon, pumpkin pie spice, and salt. Set aside.

In a small saucepan over medium heat, stir the molasses and milk for 2 to 3 minutes, or until blended. Set aside and let cool.

In a large bowl, beat the butter and brown sugar with an electric mixer on medium speed until light and fluffy. Add the eggs, one at a time, beating well after each addition. Add one-third of the flour mixture and half the milk and stir to blend. Repeat with the another third of the flour and the milk, finishing with the last third of the flour.

Transfer the batter to the prepared pan and smooth the top. Bake the cake for 45 to 50 minutes, or until a skewer inserted into the center comes out clean. Remove from the oven and let cool in the pan for 5 minutes. Invert onto a wire rack and let cool completely. Cut into squares or wedges and dust with confectioners' sugar. Serve with whipped cream or crème fraîche.

SERVES 8 TO 10

Carrot Cake

The U.K. Tea Guild named Peacocks Tea Room (Ely, Cambridgeshire) the "Top Tea Place" in 2007 due to "the very special tea experience" you find there. According to the head of the Tea Guild, "The tea menu has lots of interesting, witty, and helpful information, and the quality of the teas and the delicious sandwiches, scones, and cakes make this a 'must' on any trip to Ely." The tearoom is decorated with an interesting display of tea memorabilia and provides a library-of-sorts devoted exclusively to tea. Their carrot cake (adapted here), is one of the most popular teatime sweets, is extra yummy when it's made as a layer cake and filled and frosted all around with cream cheese icing.

CAKES

Butter for greasing

2 cups all-purpose flour

½ teaspoon baking soda

1½ teaspoons baking powder

1 teaspoon ground allspice

1 teaspoon ground cinnamon

2 cups sugar

1 cup canola oil

4 large eggs

2 cups grated carrots

ICING

12 ounces cream cheese, at room temperature

4 tablespoons unsalted butter, at room temperature

1 tablespoon vanilla extract

3 cups confectioners' sugar

Whole walnut halves for decorating (optional)

TO MAKE THE CAKES Preheat the oven to 350°F. Grease two 9-inch round cake pans and line the bottoms with wax or parchment paper.

In a large bowl, combine the flour, baking soda, baking powder, allspice, and cinnamon. Set aside. In another bowl, whisk together the sugar, oil, and eggs. Stir in the carrots. Add the oil mixture to the flour mixture and stir until blended. Spoon the batter into the prepared pans and bake for 40 to 45 minutes, or until a skewer inserted into the center comes out clean. Remove from the oven and let the cakes cool in the pans for 10 minutes on a wire rack. Invert the cakes onto the rack, then turn them upright.

TO MAKE THE ICING In a large bowl, beat the cream cheese, butter, and vanilla extract with an electric mixer until blended. Gradually beat in the confectioners' sugar and continue to beat until smooth.

Put one layer of the cake on a serving plate and spread with one-third of the icing. Top with the second layer and spread the remaining icing over the top and sides of the cake. Decorate with a ring of walnuts, if desired.

SERVES 8 TO 10

Battenberg Cake

The Westin Hotel (College Green) was created from two Dublin landmarks—Allied Irish Bank and the Pearl Building—dating to the 1860s. The Atrium, where afternoon tea is served, is housed in the former bank building and features a glass roof soaring above the five floors of the hotel. The space provides a delightful atmosphere for tea, which the chef complements with unusual and colorful sweets like Battenberg cake, a light marzipan-covered sponge cake that is made distinctive by its pink-and-white checker-board design. The origin of the name is not clear, but one theory suggests that the cake was created in honor of the marriage in 1884 of Queen Victoria's granddaughter Princess Victoria to Prince Louis of Battenberg. The four squares of the cake are said to represent the four Battenberg princes.

CAKE

½ cup (1 stick) butter, at room temperature

¾ cup granulated sugar, plus more for sprinkling

2 large eggs

1½ cups all-purpose flour

1 tablespoon baking powder

1 teaspoon almond extract

¼ cup milk

2 or 3 drops red food coloring

½ cup apricot jam, heated

One 7-ounce package marzipan (see Resources, page 171)

Confectioners' sugar for dusting

TO MAKE THE CAKE Preheat the oven to 350°F. Spray an 8-inch square baking pan with cooking oil. Dust with flour.

continued

In a large bowl, beat the butter and the ¾ cup sugar with an electric mixer on medium speed until light and fluffy. Beat in the eggs, one at a time, beating well after each addition. Fold in the flour, baking powder, almond extract, and milk.

Cut a piece of cardboard into a 7¾-by-2-inch rectangle and wrap it with aluminum foil (to serve as a barrier between the two batters). Place the separator in the center of the pan. Spread half the batter in one side of the prepared pan. Add the food coloring to the other half of the batter and stir until it's a deep pink color. Transfer the pink batter to the other half of the pan. Bake for 35 to 40 minutes, or until a skewer inserted into the center comes out clean. Remove from the oven and let cool in the pan for about 5 minutes on a wire rack. Invert the cake onto the rack to cool completely, and remove the barrier. You will have two pieces of cake.

Cut each piece of the cake in half lengthwise. Trim the crusts from the sides, ends, and tops of cakes to make evenly shaped loaves that measure about 6½-by-1½ inches. You will have some cake left over from each loaf for nibbling. Place one white and one pink strip side by side on a flat surface and spread the tops and center with the heated apricot jam to "glue" the pieces together. Place the remaining pink strip on the bottom white strip and the white strip on the bottom pink strip to create a checkerboard effect, then spread with more of the jam to adhere the pieces. Spread the top and sides of the cake with the rest of the jam.

Knead the marzipan with your hands to soften it. Dust both sides of the marzipan with confectioners' sugar and roll between sheets of waxed paper to a 12-by-7-inch rectangle. Place the cake in the center of the marzipan and bring it up over the sides of the cake so the edges meet at the top, covering the long sides but not the ends. Trim and crimp the seam and turn the cake over. With a serrated knife, trim the marzipan at the ends to make them even. Sprinkle with granulated sugar. Let the cake stand, covered, for several hours or overnight. With a serrated knife, cut the cake into 1-inch-thick slices.

SERVES 8

Victoria Sponge

Victoria sponge cake was named after the long-reigning English monarch. After the death of Prince Albert in 1861, Queen Victoria spent time at her house on the Isle of Wight, reportedly withdrawing herself from society. In order to inspire the monarch to get back into the swing of civic duties, she was encouraged to host tea parties, at which a sponge cake was served. "Victoria sponges" became fashionable throughout Victorian England and also became the measure of the home baker. A traditional Victoria sponge consists of jam and whipped cream sandwiched between two sponge cakes. The top of the cake is generally not iced or decorated, except for a sprinkling of confectioners' sugar, sometimes done over a doily to create a lacy pattern. At London's Brown's Hotel (30 Abermarle Street), where afternoon tea is an institution, this sponge is always on the sweets trolley.

CAKE	FILLING
1 cup (2 sticks) butter, at room temperature	5 tablespoons butter, at room temperature
1 cup sugar	½ teaspoon vanilla extract
1 teaspoon vanilla extract	1½ cups confectioners' sugar, plus more for dusting
Pinch of salt	
1 tablespoon grated lemon zest	2½ teaspoons milk
4 large eggs	½ cup strawberry jam
2 cups self-rising flour	
	Fresh strawberries for garnish (optional)

continued

TO MAKE THE CAKE Preheat the oven to 325°F. Spray a 9-inch round pan with cooking oil. Dust with flour.

In a medium bowl, cream the butter and sugar with an electric mixer on medium speed until light and fluffy. Beat in the vanilla, salt, and lemon zest. Add the eggs, one at a time, beating well after each addition. Whisk in the flour until smooth.

Transfer the batter to the prepared pan and bake for 30 to 35 minutes, or until the top is golden and a skewer inserted into the center comes out clean. Remove from the oven and let cool in the pan for 15 minutes on a wire rack.

TO MAKE THE FILLING Beat the butter and vanilla with an electric mixer until smooth. Beat in the 1½ cups sugar a little at a time. Beat in the milk and continue to beat until light and fluffy.

Invert the cake onto a serving plate, then turn it upright. Cut it in half horizontally and spread the bottom half with the jam. Spread the filling over the jam and place the top half of the cake on it cut side down. Lightly sift confectioners' sugar over the top. Cover and refrigerate the cake for 1 hour before serving. Garnish with fresh strawberries, if desired.

SERVES 8

Snow White Cupcakes

In its June 2008 "Hotel Issue," *Travel & Leisure* magazine named the Milestone (1 Kensington Court) the top hotel overall for service. Located across from Kensington Park and Palace, it's one of the loveliest hotels in the Royal Borough of Kensington and Chelsea. The hotel staff takes pride in its afternoon tea service, which always includes these decadent cupcakes (adapted here). Ask for a table by the window in the Park Lounge for fabulous views of the park and the palace beyond.

CUPCAKES	ICING
2½ cups all-purpose flour	½ cup (1 stick) unsalted butter, at room temperature
1 tablespoon baking powder	
4 large eggs, separated	3 cups confectioners' sugar
1¼ cups sugar	4 to 6 tablespoons milk
⅔ cup warm water	½ teaspoon vanilla extract
⅔ cup canola oil	
1½ teaspoons vanilla extract	

TO MAKE THE CUPCAKES Preheat the oven to 350°F. Line a 12-cup muffin tin with paper liners.

In a small bowl, sift together the flour and baking powder. Set aside. In a large bowl, beat the egg whites with an electric mixer on high speed until soft peaks form. Continue to beat, adding the sugar in three additions, beating well after each additon. Fold the flour mixture into the egg whites. In a medium bowl, beat in the egg yolks, water, oil, and vanilla with an electric mixer on medium speed until smooth. Fold into the whites mixture.

Divide the batter evenly among the muffin cups. Bake for 20 to 23 minutes, or until a tooth-pick inserted into the center of each comes out clean. Remove from the oven and let cool for 10 minutes in the pan, then transfer to a wire rack to cool. Reline the cups and repeat with the remaining batter.

TO MAKE THE ICING In a large bowl, beat the butter and sugar with an electric mixer on medium until light and fluffy. With the mixer on low speed, add 4 tablespoons of the milk and the vanilla and beat until smooth. Beat in the remaining 2 tablespoons milk for a smoother consistency, if desired. Spread or pipe the icing on the tops of the cupcakes.

MAKES 18 CUPCAKES

Bakewell Tarts

Ashford Castle (Cong, County Mayo), one of Ireland's most famous properties, was transformed from a thirteenth-century castle into a castle hotel in 1915. At one time under the ownership of the Guinness family, it will always be associated with their name, especially Lord and Lady Ardilaun, who enjoyed one of the great romances of their time while living there. In celebration of their twenty-fifth wedding anniversary, they received a gift of a beautiful silver tea service, still on display in the foyer. In recognition of their love of afternoon tea, guests today enjoy "Lord and Lady Ardilaun's Afternoon Tea" served in the traditional fashion in the Drawing Room. These raspberry jam and almond filled tarts (adapted here), named for the English village of Bakewell where they originated, are one of the castle's most popular teatime sweets.

PASTRY	FILLING
1 cup all-purpose flour	½ cup raspberry jam
2 tablespoons sugar	½ cup (1 stick) unsalted butter
½ teaspoon salt	1 cup superfine sugar
6 tablespoons unsalted butter, cold and cut into small pieces, plus more for greasing	2 tablespoons grated lemon zest
	2 large eggs, beaten
2 large egg yolks	½ cup all-purpose flour, sifted
½ teaspoon vanilla extract	½ cup ground almonds
1 to 2 tablespoons cold water	¼ cup slivered almonds
	Confectioners' sugar for dusting

TO MAKE THE PASTRY Combine the flour, sugar, and salt in a food processor. Pulse 1 or 2 times. Add the 6 tablespoons butter, a few pieces at a time, and pulse in 1-second increments until the mixture resembles coarse crumbs. Add the egg yolks, vanilla, and water and process until the dough comes together. Turn the dough out onto a work surface and form it into a ball. Wrap it in plastic wrap and refrigerate for at least 30 minutes.

Preheat the oven to 375°F. Lightly butter two 12-cup mini-muffin pans. Dust a work surface with flour.

Flatten the dough into a disk, cut it in half, and roll out each into a ¼-inch-thick circle. With a 2-inch round biscuit cutter, cut out 12 rounds of pastry from each half. Put each round in a muffin cup and gently press the dough into the cup. Discard any pastry scraps.

TO MAKE THE FILLING Put 1 teaspoon jam into each pastry-lined cup. Combine the butter, superfine sugar, and lemon zest in a food processor and process for 20 to 30 seconds, or until light and fluffy. Add the beaten eggs. Add the flour and ground almonds and process 10 to 20 seconds, or until well blended. Spoon the mixture over the jam so that each cup is three-quarters full. Sprinkle with the slivered almonds.

Bake the tartlets for 23 to 25 minutes, or until golden. Remove from the oven and let cool in the pan for 10 minutes on a wire rack. Remove the tartlets from the pans and dust with confectioners' sugar.

MAKES 2 DOZEN TARTLETS

Lemon Cream Tartlets with Wild Forest Berries

Lemon tarts are the keynote desserts of many European teatime sweet spreads, and ones like these, which are served at teatime aboard *Serenity* and *Symphony*, the ships of Crystal Cruise Lines (see page 157), turn up everywhere. In this recipe the chef uses sweet-tart wild raspberries as a perfect counterpoint to the silkiness of the lemon cream, but you can substitute local berries with equally good results. The ground pistachio garnish adds color, flavor, and texture to the otherwise simple tart, and the chocolate lining adds an element of surprise.

PASTRY	LEMON CREAM FILLING
1¾ cups all-purpose flour	4 large egg yolks
2 tablespoons sugar	½ cup sugar
Pinch of salt	1 cup milk
½ cup (1 stick) unsalted butter, cold and cut into small pieces, plus more for greasing	1 tablespoon granulated gelatin
	Grated zest and juice of 1 lemon
1 large egg	1 cup heavy whipping cream
1 tablespoon ice water	2 ounces (2 squares) dark chocolate, melted
	2 cups wild raspberries
	¼ cup seedless raspberry jam, heated
	¼ cup ground pistachios

continued

TO MAKE THE PASTRY Put the flour, sugar, salt, and the ½ cup butter in a food processor. Process for 10 to 15 seconds, or until the mixture resembles coarse crumbs. Add the egg and water and process for 5 to 10 seconds, or until the dough just comes together. Dust a work surface with flour. Turn out the dough, form it into a ball, and divide it in half. Wrap each in plastic wrap and refrigerate for at least 30 minutes.

Preheat the oven to 325°F. Butter two 12-well tartlet pans.

Roll each piece of the dough out into a ⅛-inch-thick circle. Using a 3-inch round biscuit cutter, cut out 10 to 12 rounds from each. Fit each into a tartlet pan and cover with a small square of parchment paper or aluminum foil. Fill with dried beans or pie weights. Discard any pastry scraps.

Bake for 18 to 20 minutes, or until lightly browned. Remove from the oven and let cool for about 10 minutes on a wire rack. Remove the beans and paper.

TO MAKE THE FILLING In a medium bowl, beat the egg yolks and ¼ cup of the sugar with an electric mixer on medium speed until pale and thick. In a small saucepan over medium heat, bring the milk, the remaining ¼ cup sugar, and the gelatin to a boil. Gradually whisk the milk mixture into the yolk mixture. Return to the saucepan and cook, stirring constantly, for 3 to 5 minutes, or until bubbles form around the edge of the pan. Strain the mixture through a fine-mesh sieve into a bowl, stir in the lemon zest and juice, and press a piece of plastic wrap directly onto the surface to prevent a skin from forming. Refrigerate for 18 to 20 minutes, or until the mixture thickens. In a small bowl, whip the cream with an electric mixer on high speed until soft peaks form. Fold into the lemon mixture.

With a pastry brush, coat the inside of the pastry shells with a thin layer of melted chocolate. Allow the chocolate to set. Divide the lemon cream among the tart shells and refrigerate for 15 minutes. Arrange the berries on top of the filling. With a clean pastry brush, coat the raspberries with the heated jam, then sprinkle with the pistachios.

MAKES 20 TO 22 TARTLETS

VARIATIONS

Lemon Curd Tartlets with Seasonal Berries

Bodysgallen Hall (Llandudno) provides the best in Welsh country house hospitality. The hotel is at the end of a winding drive through wooded parkland and formal gardens with fabulous views of the Snowdonia range of mountains and the medieval castle at Conwy. For afternoon tea, the chef uses seasonal berries to top these tarts filled with lemon curd, that can also be used with scones.

Prepare the tartlet shells as directed.

NOTE To make lemon curd, combine 2¼ cups sugar, the grated zest and juice of 4 lemons, 1 cup (2 sticks) unsalted butter, and 6 large eggs in the top of a double boiler set over simmering water. Whisk for 10 to 15 minutes, or until the mixture is thick and smooth. Let the lemon curd cool. Fill the tart shells with the lemon curd. Arrange one or more types of berries on top and dust with confectioners' sugar.

MAKES 20 TO 22 TARTLETS

continued

Queen of Hearts Tartlets

The Mandeville Hotel (Mandeville Place) is located in London's fashionable Marylebone Village within a few minutes' walk of some of Mayfair's most exciting stores, art galleries, antique shops, and auction houses like Sotheby's and Christie's. Great design and high style are the keys to the hotel, right down to the fashionable afternoon designer tea presented on china by Zandra Rhodes (see pages 63 and 81).

Prepare the tartlet shells as directed.

In a large bowl, whisk together 4 eggs and 1 cup sugar until smooth. Stir in the grated zest and juice of 4 lemons. Whisk in ½ cup heavy whipping cream. Pour into the prepared pastry shells and bake for 35 to 40 minutes, or until the filling is set. Remove from the oven and let cool for 1 hour on a wire rack. Dust with confectioners' sugar and serve with a spoonful of Crème Fraîche (see Note, page 30), if desired.

MAKES 20 TO 22 TARTLETS

NOTE If you prefer to use prepared pastry, Clearbrook Farms makes sweet butter tart shells in 1¾-inch and 3-inch sizes that are ready for filling (see Resources, page 173).

BITE-SIZE TARTS : SIMPLE SHELLS, FABULOUS FILLINGS

ANY AFTERNOON TEA worth noting will offer bite-size tartlets made with homemade pastry and filled with custard, cream cheese, fruit, or chocolate. If you're intimidated by the thought of making your own pastry—or simply don't have time—here are two easy-as-pie recipes that start with prepared shells and finish with no-bake fillings. Serve them at your next tea party without ever having to touch a rolling pin.

BUTTER TARTS WITH ORANGE-MANGO CURD

In a small saucepan over medium heat, whisk together 3 large eggs, ¾ cup sugar, and ½ cup orange-mango juice, such as Tropicana brand. Cook, whisking constantly, for 8 to 10 minutes, or until the mixture starts to boil and thicken. Pour the mixture through a fine-mesh sieve into a bowl and place a piece of plastic wrap directly on the surface to prevent a skin from forming. Refrigerate for 2 hours or up to 1 day. Divide among 48 Clearbrook Farms mini bite-size sweet tart shells and top each with a single raspberry or blueberry. Serve immediately or refrigerate for up to 4 hours.

MAKES 48 TARTS

PHYLLO TARTS WITH STRAWBERRY CREAM AND PISTACHIOS

In a medium bowl, beat 8 ounces softened cream cheese, 2 tablespoons granulated brown sugar, the grated zest and juice of 1 small orange, and 1 tablespoon chopped fresh mint with an electric mixer until smooth. Pipe or spoon the filling into 30 Athens mini phyllo shells, top with a single strawberry, stem-side down, and sprinkle with 4 tablespoons chopped pistachios. Serve immediately or refrigerate for up to 4 hours.

MAKES 30 TARTS

Taffy Apples Bavarois

Taffy Apples is a Celtic-style cider from Tomos Watkin, a Welsh brewer of distinctive beers, ales, and ciders; *bavarois* (pronounced bah-vah-RWAH) is a rich custard to which gelatin and whipped cream are added. Together they're deliciously compatible in this apple-flavored teatime treat from Morgans (Somerset Place), a unique boutique hotel built within what was once Swansea's Victorian Port Authority building. The custard rests on a crust made with oaty digestive biscuits.

CUSTARD

1 cup Taffy Apples cider or similar hard cider

½ cup apple juice

2½ cups milk

1½ teaspoons granulated gelatin

4 large eggs

½ cup superfine sugar

2 cups heavy whipping cream

BASE

1½ cups biscuit crumbs from McVitie's HobNobs or Carr's Digestives (see Resources, pages 172 and 170, respectively)

½ cup (1 stick) unsalted butter, melted

1 tablespoon finely grated lemon zest

Canola oil for the ring molds

TO MAKE THE CUSTARD In a small saucepan over medium heat, combine the cider and apple juice. Cook for 10 to 15 minutes, or until reduced by half. Set aside.

Put the milk in a small bowl and sprinkle the gelatin over it to soften for a few minutes. In a medium saucepan over medium-low heat, whisk together the eggs and sugar. Whisk in the milk and cook, stirring constantly, for 5 to 7 minutes, or until the mixture is thick enough to coat the back of a metal spoon (about 160°F on an instant-read thermometer). Remove from the heat and cool quickly by placing the pan in a bowl filled with ice. Stir in the reduced cider. Press a piece of plastic wrap directly on the surface of the custard to prevent a skin from forming and let stand in the ice for 15 minutes. Remove from the ice and refrigerate for 30 minutes.

Whip the cream with an electric mixer on high speed until soft peaks form. Fold the whipped cream into the custard until blended.

TO MAKE THE BASE Preheat the oven to 325°F. Lightly oil eight 3-inch ring molds and put them on a baking sheet.

In a small bowl, combine the biscuit crumbs, butter, and lemon zest. Press the mixture into the molds and bake for 8 to 10 minutes, or until the crusts are set. Remove from the oven and let cool on a wire rack.

Spoon the custard over each crust and refrigerate for 4 to 6 hours, or until set.

Run a knife around the molds to loosen and gently lift off the rings. Place each pudding on a serving plate.

SERVES 8

Twinings Lady Grey Cookies

Twinings, one of Britain's most revered tea companies, celebrated its three-hundredth anniversary in 2006 with a round of special events and a selection of recipes that highlight tea in cooking. These tea-flavored butter cookies are a good example. For more on Twinings, see page 39.

4 Twinings Lady Grey tea bags	1 large egg
¼ cup boiling water	½ teaspoon grated lemon zest
½ cup (1 stick) unsalted butter, at room temperature	1½ cups all-purpose flour
½ cup granulated sugar	½ teaspoon baking powder
	Confectioners' sugar for dusting

In a small bowl, combine the tea bags and boiling water. Let steep for 3 minutes, and with a spoon, press firmly on the tea bags to extract maximum flavor. Remove and discard the tea bags. Set the tea concentrate aside.

In a large bowl, beat the butter and sugar with an electric mixer on medium speed until light and fluffy.

Beat in the egg and lemon zest. Add the tea concentrate, flour, and baking powder, then beat on low speed until a soft dough forms. Form the dough into a 1½-inch-thick log, wrap in plastic wrap, and refrigerate for 6 to 12 hours, or until firm.

Preheat the oven to 350°F.

Remove the dough from the refrigerator. Place on a clean work surface, cut the log into ½-inch-thick slices, and place on a baking sheet. Bake for 15 to 18 minutes, or until the cookies are lightly browned. Remove from the oven and let cool on a wire rack. Dust with confectioners' sugar.

MAKES ABOUT 16 COOKIES

Passion Fruit Posset with Strawberry Jelly

The Palm Court Lounge is one of the most elegant spaces in London's Park Lane Hotel (Piccadilly), and hand-painted murals, polished service, and the resident harpist add to the ambience of having afternoon tea here. With five tea menus to choose from—Traditional, Art Deco, Krug Champagne, Chocolate, and special occasion teas like the English Rose (offered in spring)—you'll be spoiled for choice. An interesting twist to the menu is this "posset," an old-fashioned drink that doubles as a dessert when the cream is heated and thickened. Here the chef tops the little puddings with homemade strawberry jelly and serves them in small glasses. Shot glasses or 4-ounce cordial glasses are perfect.

POSSET	STRAWBERRY JELLY
2 cups heavy whipping cream	2 cups strawberries, hulled and quartered
½ cup superfine sugar	⅓ cup superfine sugar
⅔ cup passion fruit juice (see Note)	1 teaspoon granulated gelatin
	Clotted Cream (page 60) or Crème Fraîche (see Note, page 30) for serving

TO MAKE THE POSSET In a medium saucepan over medium heat, combine the cream and sugar. Bring to a boil and cook, stirring constantly, for 3 to 5 minutes, or until slightly reduced. Add the passion fruit juice, return to a gentle boil, and cook for 1 minute longer. Remove from the heat and fill eight 3-ounce glasses two-thirds full. Let cool for 15 minutes, then refrigerate for 8 to 10 hours, or until set.

continued

TO MAKE THE JELLY Combine the strawberries and sugar in a metal bowl and wrap with plastic wrap. Place the bowl over a saucepan of gently simmering water without allowing the bowl to come into contact with the water, and leave for about 60 minutes, or until the strawberry juice is released. Pour the strawberries and juice into a fine-mesh sieve set over a bowl to catch the juices. Refrigerate and let drain overnight. Discard the strawberries. (You should have about ½ cup juice.)

Warm the juice in the microwave, then stir in the gelatin until it dissolves. Pour a thin layer of jelly onto the puddings and return to the refrigerator to set. Serve with a dollop of cream.

SERVES 8

NOTE If you have trouble finding passion fruit juice, you can substitute pomegranate juice.

The French Art of Tea

Pastries and cakes from Ladurée—which counts shops and tea parlors in Paris, London, Monaco, Geneva, and Lausanne—come smartly wrapped with signature ribbons like these at the Rue Bonaparte location.

I raised to my lips a spoonful of the tea in which I had soaked a morsel of the cake. No sooner had the warm liquid mixed with the crumbs touched my palate than a shiver ran through me and I stopped, intent upon the extraordinary thing that was happening to me. An exquisite pleasure had invaded my senses . . . when could it have come to me, this all-powerful joy? I sensed that it was connected with the taste of the tea and the cake, but that it infinitely transcended those savors.

MARCEL PROUST, FRENCH NOVELIST

REGARDLESS OF the setting for afternoon tea, French pastries—rich fruit and chocolate tarts, crisp madeleines, fragile Mille-Feuilles, and perfectly shaped *macarons*—are an integral part of the ritual. And why not?

The French have elevated *pâtisserie* to an art form and its popularity was established long before that of tea drinking.

Surprisingly, while France is considered a coffee-drinking country, Paris—not

London—is actually the tearoom capital of the world with more than 150 tearooms located throughout the city. Unlike the three-course British afternoon tea ritual, a classic "French tea" consists simply of a pot of perfectly prepared tea and a *pâtisserie*, or pastry, of your choice. Here, the two share equal billing, with the *pâtisserie* as important as the tea.

After its introduction to Europe in the seventeenth century, tea was especially popular in France. It first arrived in Paris around 1636 (more than twenty years before it appeared in England) and quickly became popular among the aristocracy because of its purported medicinal qualities. For a time following the French Revolution, however, tea, long associated with royalty, went out of fashion. But a mere fifty years later, everything English was the rage

again, and it became stylish to take tea, often in the evening after dinner and accompanied by small pastries.

It was around this time that the Mariage brothers, Henri and Edouard, began to expand their family's tea import business. In June 1854, they founded Mariage Frères Tea Company in Paris, today the oldest in France. Mariage Frères quickly demonstrated what has become its trademark—interesting blends—and their current catalogue lists about 200 blends among its selection of more than 500 teas. They also sell tea-flavored cookies, tea candy, and tea jellies, and their tearooms are counted among the finest in Paris.

Today, tea drinking is quite popular in France, especially in Paris, and French tea drinkers pride themselves on their diverse tastes, enjoying English-style blends, Japanese greens, and Chinese

In Paris, even the Metro signs are stylishly decorated in filigree ironwork and Art Nouveau lamps.

The Mariage Fréres tea shop on Rue du Bourg-Tibourg is one of the oldest in Paris.

whites. They practice what they call the "French art of tea," which simply consists of quality ingredients, careful preparation, and elegant presentation. A marked interest in teas grown on specific estates—similar to the French devotion to wines grown in particular areas—is another hallmark of the French approach to tea.

The history of Parisian tearooms is also intimately entwined with that of the Ladurée family, especially Louis Ernest Ladurée, a miller from the southwest of France. He is generally credited with their foundation, when he opened a bakery at 16 Rue Royale in 1862. In the 1870s, Baron Haussmann was changing the face of Paris when a fire destroyed Ladurée's bakery. When Ladurée rebuilt it, he transformed it into a pastry shop and commissioned a well-known fin-de-siècle painter and poster artist to decorate the new shop with elaborate murals and paintings.

As cafés developed during the Second Empire, Ladurée's wife decided to mix styles and combine the café with the cake shop, thus giving birth to one of the first *salons de thé* in Paris. The tearoom had an advantage over Parisian cafés as it could welcome ladies without causing a stir, and today, Ladurée tearooms—four in Paris, one in Geneva, one in Monaco, one in Lausanne, and two in London (a full-service tearoom in Harrods and a small pâtisserie on Piccadilly)—continue the reputation established by its founder and are the great centers for pastry creation in Europe. There are more than 150 tearooms in Paris today ranging from unpretentious neighborhood cafés to grand salons in gilded belle époque hotels.

This Ladurée salon de thé at 21 Rue Bonaparte is one of four located in Paris. Like the others, it is beautifully decorated with elaborate murals and paintings.

Madeleines

Madeleines are small cakelike cookies that are baked in molds that give them a delicate shell shape. According to one story, the name "madeleine" was given to the cookies by Louis XV to honor his father-in-law's cook, Madeleine Paulmier. Louis first tasted them at the Château Commercy in Lorraine in 1755, and his wife, Marie, introduced them to the court at Versailles where they soon became all the rage. Whatever the origins, they have become inextricably linked with the author Marcel Proust, who, in his *Remembrances of Things Past*, called the madeleine, "a little shell of cake, so generously sensual beneath the piety of its stern pleating." At the Ritz Hôtel (15 Place Vendôme), where afternoon tea is served in the elegant Bar Vendôme, these cookies (adapted here) are called "Madeleines de Proust" in honor of the writer who so loved them. The chef gives them a distinctive citrus flavor with the addition of lemon and orange zest, but you'll also find them flavored with pistachios, tea, and chocolate (see Variation, page 142).

½ cup (1 stick) unsalted butter	Pinch of salt
3 large eggs	⅓ cup honey
½ cup granulated sugar	1 teaspoon grated lemon zest
¾ cup all-purpose flour	1 teaspoon grated orange zest
¼ cup ground blanched almonds (optional)	
½ teaspoon baking powder	Confectioners' sugar for dusting

continued

In a small saucepan over medium heat, melt the butter. Set aside.

In a large bowl, beat the eggs and sugar with an electric mixer on medium speed until light and fluffy. Stir in the flour, almonds, if using, baking powder, and salt and beat for 3 to 5 minutes, or until well blended. Stir in the honey, melted butter, and lemon and orange zests. Cover the batter with a piece of plastic wrap and refrigerate for 3 to 4 hours or up to 1 day.

Preheat the oven to 325°F. Spray two 12-well madeleine pans with cooking oil. Dust with flour.

Spoon 1 rounded tablespoon of the batter into each well (they will be about two-thirds full). Bake in the upper and lower thirds of the oven, switching the position of the pans halfway through baking, for 20 to 25 minutes, or until golden around the edges. Remove from the oven and let cool for 5 minutes on a wire rack. Invert the pans to remove the cookies and dust with confectioners' sugar.

MAKES 2 DOZEN COOKIES

VARIATION

Chocolate Madeleines

Substitute 3 tablespoons Dutch-processed cocoa powder and 1 ounce (1 square) bittersweet (not unsweetened) chocolate, melted and cooled, for the almonds and lemon and orange zests. Proceed with the recipe as directed. Stir in the cocoa powder and chocolate with the honey and butter.

Earl Grey Imperial Madeleines

At Mariage Frères tearoom (30 Rue du Bourg-Tibourg) in the Marais district, the dessert cart is called the "Pâtisserie Chariot Colonial." It's laden with *macarons*, sweet biscuits, croissants, tarts, and these "imperial" madeleines infused with Earl Grey tea.

½ cup (1 stick) unsalted butter

2 tablespoons Mariage Frères Earl Grey Imperial loose tea or 4 Earl Grey tea bags

2 large eggs

¼ cup superfine sugar

1 cup all-purpose flour

1½ teaspoons baking powder

Pinch of salt

¼ cup honey

In a small saucepan over medium heat, melt the butter. Add the loose tea or tea bags to the melted butter and let sit for about 5 minutes. Strain the butter through a fine-mesh sieve; with a spoon, press on the tea bags to extract maximum flavor. Discard the tea bags and set aside.

In a large bowl, beat the eggs and sugar with an electric mixer on medium speed until light and fluffy. Stir in the flour, baking powder, and salt. Stir the strained butter into the batter. Stir in the honey. Cover with a piece of plastic wrap and refrigerate the batter for 3 to 4 hours or up to 1 day.

Preheat the oven to 400°F. Spray two 12-well madeleine pans with cooking oil. Dust with flour.

Spoon 1 rounded tablespoon of the batter into each well (they should be about two-thirds full). Bake in the upper and lower thirds of the oven for 10 to 12 minutes, or until the cookies are golden, switching the position of the pans halfway through baking. Remove from the oven and let cool for 5 minutes on a wire rack. Invert the pans to remove the cookies.

MAKES 2 DOZEN COOKIES

Pierre Hermé's Chocolate-Filled Macarons

Fourth-generation pastry chef Pierre Hermé is renowned for his innovative and unusual French pastry creations. He is the owner of two pastry boutiques in Paris and five in Tokyo (see A Traveler's Guide to European Tearooms for addresses), and his *macarons* are legendary. He enjoys experimenting with flavors and produces simple *macarons* flavored with chocolate, hazelnut, and chestnut, and more exotic ones made with rose, lychee, and raspberries that he calls "Ispahan." *Macarons* made with bananas, passion fruit, ginger, and hazelnuts are called "Arabella." For mere mortals, we can be content with the flavor of these light and chewy ones filled with chocolate, which are perfect for tea. You should make the filling for the *macarons* at least one day ahead to thicken it.

CHOCOLATE FILLING	MACARONS
¾ cup whole milk	One 1-pound box confectioners' sugar
5 tablespoons unsalted butter	2 cups whole blanched almonds
8 ounces bittersweet (not unsweetened) or semisweet chocolate, finely chopped	6 tablespoons unsweetened cocoa powder
	6 large egg whites (about ¾ cup)

TO MAKE THE FILLING In a medium saucepan over medium heat, combine the milk and butter. Bring to a simmer and remove from the heat. Add the chocolate and whisk until melted and smooth. Transfer to a small bowl and let cool completely. Cover and refrigerate for 24 hours or up to 3 days, or until thick and cold.

continued

TO MAKE THE MACARONS Preheat the oven to 400°F. Line 2 large baking sheets with parchment paper.

Combine the confectioners' sugar and almonds in a food processor and process for 5 to 6 minutes, scraping down the sides of the bowl often, or until the nuts are ground to a fine powder. Add the cocoa and process 1 minute more, or until combined. In a large bowl, beat the egg whites with an electric mixer on medium speed until stiff peaks form. Fold the nut mixture into the whites in 4 additions, making a thick batter.

Spoon half the batter into a pastry bag fitted with a ½-inch plain tip. Pipe the batter onto a prepared sheet in 12 walnut-size mounds, spacing the mounds 1 inch apart. Bake one sheet at a time for 10 to 11 minutes, or until firm to the touch in the center and dry and cracked on top. Remove from the oven and slide the parchment with cookies onto a work surface to cool completely. Repeat with the remaining batter, cooling the baking sheet completely and lining with clean parchment for each batch.

Arrange 12 *macarons*, flat-side up, on a work surface. Drop 1 scant tablespoon of filling onto each cookie, then top with a second *macaron*, flat-side down. Press lightly to adhere. Repeat with the remaining cookies. Arrange on a platter, cover, and refrigerate for at least 2 hours or up to 1 day. Serve chilled.

MAKES 2 DOZEN MACARONS

Petit Pains au Chocolat

Pain au chocolat, called a *chocolatine* in certain regions of France, is made with puff pastry wrapped around small bars of chocolate. Translated literally as "bread with chocolate," *pain au chocolat* is a variation of a croissant and is typically eaten for breakfast or with afternoon tea. For best results in this recipe (and for all chocolate baking), use a couverture-style chocolate (the name given to chocolate containing not less than 32 percent cocoa butter). These perfect-for-tea size *petit pains* are a snap to make with frozen puff pastry.

2 sheets frozen puff pastry (from a 17-ounce package), such as Pepperidge Farm brand	Four 3½-ounce bars imported bittersweet or milk chocolate, each cut into six 2¾-inch pieces
1 large egg	Sugar for sprinkling
1 tablespoon water	

Preheat the oven to 400°F. Line 2 baking sheets with parchment paper.

Thaw the pastry at room temperature for 40 minutes. Unfold on a lightly floured surface and cut each sheet into 12 squares. Beat the egg with the water and brush the top of each square with the egg glaze. Place 1 chocolate piece on the edge of a pastry square. Roll up tightly, enclosing the chocolate. Repeat with the remaining pastry and chocolate. Place the pastry rolls, seam-side down, on the prepared sheets. (Can be made 1 day ahead. Cover with plastic wrap and refrigerate. Cover and refrigerate the remaining egg glaze.)

Brush the tops of the pastry rolls with the remaining egg glaze. Sprinkle lightly with sugar. Bake for about 15 minutes, or until golden brown. Serve warm or at room temperature.

MAKES 2 DOZEN PASTRIES

Sokoto Moelleux au Chocolat

This traditional French chocolate cake has a velvety molten chocolate center that flows seductively onto your plate the moment it's touched with a fork. The chef at Geneva's Hôtel d'Angleterre (17 Quai de Mont Blanc) named the dish after Sokoto, a town in Nigeria where the cocoa beans originate for this 58 percent pure chocolate. He serves it with homemade passion fruit and banana sorbet and mango coulis as a dessert, but for afternoon tea, you can serve it simply with a dollop of whipped cream, some fresh raspberries or strawberries, or with a purée of fruits.

5 ounces Sokoto or other couverture-style chocolate

½ cup (1 stick) unsalted butter

4 large eggs

1 cup sugar

1 cup all-purpose flour

Whipped cream, for serving (optional)

Fresh berries, for serving (optional)

Fruit coulis for serving (optional)

Preheat the oven to 350°F. Spray eight 4-ounce ramekins with cooking oil spray with flour.

In a small saucepan over medium heat, melt the chocolate with the butter. In a medium bowl, beat the eggs and sugar with an electric mixer on medium speed until light and fluffy. Stir in the flour and chocolate mixture. Transfer the batter to the prepared ramekins and bake for 10 minutes, or until the tops are firm. Run a knife around the sides of the ramekins and invert the cakes onto serving plates. Top with whipped cream, fresh berries, or fruit coulis, if desired. Serve immediately.

SERVES 8

Chocolate-Hazelnut Pots de Crème

While pastries, tarts, and rich *gâteau* (the French word for "cake") are typically served at *pâtisseries* and tea salons, you might also find *pot de crème* (French for "pot of cream"), a rich custard or chocolate dessert served in a tiny china or ceramic cup. To double the pleasure, try serving this hazelnut-infused chocolate mixture in its own chocolate pot. Astor Chocolate makes Belgian chocolate liqueur cups, shells, and other chocolate products that are perfect for filling with cream, mousse, or ice cream.

⅔ cup heavy whipping cream

⅓ cup milk

7 ounces (7 squares) bittersweet chocolate, broken into pieces

2 large egg yolks

3 to 4 tablespoons Frangelico or other hazelnut liqueur

2 tablespoons unsalted butter, at room temperature

60 mini chocolate cups, such as Astor brand (see Resources, page 170)

60 whole hazelnuts

In a small saucepan over medium heat, heat the cream and milk until just boiling. Remove from the heat, add the chocolate, and stir until the chocolate is melted and smooth. Beat in the egg yolks, Frangelico, and butter until smooth. Divide the chocolate mixture among the chocolate cups and refrigerate for 60 minutes.

Top each one with a hazelnut and refrigerate again for 2 hours, or until the chocolate is completely set. (Can be made in advance and stored in the refrigerator for up to 1 week. Leftover chocolate can be frozen for later use.)

MAKES 60 CUPS

Petite Blueberry Cakes

Hôtel Le Bristol (112 Rue de Faubourg Saint-Honoré) opened as a hotel in April 1925. Today the Bar is the venue for the hotel's "Fashion Teas" (see page 63), where haute couture meets afternoon tea and, quite possibly, small blueberry cakes like these will be served.

½ cup (1 stick) plus 2 tablespoons unsalted butter, at room temperature

1 cup granulated sugar

2 large eggs, separated

2½ cups all-purpose flour

2 teaspoons baking powder

1 cup milk

1 cup blueberries

Confectioners' sugar for dusting

Preheat the oven to 350°F. Spray a fluted or Bundt muffin pan (see Note) with cooking oil spray with flour.

In a large bowl, beat the butter and sugar with an electric mixer on medium speed until light and fluffy.

Beat in the egg yolks, flour, and baking powder. Beat for 1 to 2 minutes, beat in the milk and egg whites, and continue to beat until smooth.

Put 5 or 6 blueberries in each of the muffin cups, then spoon about 1 tablespoon of the batter into each. Bake for 16 to 18 minutes, or until a skewer inserted into the center of each comes out clean. Remove from the oven and let cool for 10 minutes on a wire rack. Invert the pan onto the rack to release the cakes. Regrease and flour the pan and repeat with the remaining blueberries and batter. Dust the tops of the cakes with confectioners' sugar just before serving.

MAKES 2 DOZEN SMALL CAKES

NOTE Nordic Ware makes a Bundt brownie pan that's perfect for these little cakes.

Religieuse Chocolat

The Hôtel de Crillon, overlooking historic Place de la Concorde, occupies one of the most exceptional locations in Paris. At teatime, the chef rolls out enviable French pastries, including *religieuse* (French for "the nun"), two cream-filled pastry puffs—a small one stacked on top of a larger one and resembling a nun's bonnet. Cream puff pastry, also known as *pâte à choux* or choux paste, is the basis for many French desserts including *religieuse*. Adapted here, the four-part recipe is an impressive teatime sweet.

Crème Pâtissière (see page 94)

CHOUX PASTE

½ cup (1 stick) unsalted butter,
cut into small pieces

2 teaspoons superfine sugar

¼ teaspoon salt

1 cup water

1¼ cups all-purpose flour

4 large eggs

1 egg beaten with 1 teaspoon water

CHOCOLATE FONDANT

¼ cup water

1 tablespoon light corn syrup

1 ounce (1 square) semisweet chocolate

3 cups confectioners' sugar

½ teaspoon vanilla extract

ICING

4 tablespoons unsalted butter,
at room temperature

½ cup confectioners' sugar

The day before you plan to serve these, prepare the Crème Pâtissière. Cover with plastic wrap and refrigerate.

TO MAKE THE CHOUX PASTE On the day of baking, preheat the oven to 400°F. Line 2 baking sheets with parchment paper.

In a large saucepan over medium heat, bring the butter, sugar, salt, and water to a boil and then remove from the heat. Add the flour all at once and stir rapidly with a wooden spoon until the dough starts to pull away from the sides of the pan. Let the mixture cool for 4 to 5 minutes.

Beat in the eggs one at a time, stirring well after each addition. Continue to beat until the mixture is smooth and shiny. With 2 teaspoons, form 8 small balls of dough and place them on a prepared pan. With 2 tablespoons, form 8 large balls and place them on the other pan. Brush each with the egg and water glaze.

Bake the small cream puffs for 23 to 25 minutes and the large ones for 28 to 30 minutes, or until puffed and golden brown. Remove from the oven and let cool for 10 to 15 minutes on a wire rack. (Cream puffs can be made 1 day ahead and reheated in a 350°F oven for 4 to 5 minutes.)

Cut each cream puff in half horizontally with a serrated knife. Spoon or pipe the *crème pâtissière* into each one and replace the top.

TO MAKE THE FONDANT In a small saucepan over medium heat, combine the water, corn syrup, and chocolate. Cook for 4 to 5 minutes, or until the chocolate melts. Stir in the sugar and vanilla and cook for 8 to 10 minutes, or until the temperature reaches 95°F on a candy thermometer. The fondant should be thin enough to be poured but thick enough to glaze.

Spoon 1 tablespoon of the fondant over the top of each large cream puff and immediately place a smaller one on top (the fondant will "glue" them together). Spoon the remaining fondant over the small ones.

TO MAKE THE ICING Cream the butter and sugar with an electric mixer on medium speed until smooth. Fill a piping bag fitted with a star tip with the icing, then pipe 8 to 10 lines from the top of the large cream puff to the top of the small one to "connect" the two. Refrigerate until serving time.

MAKES 8 PASTRIES

Saint-Honoré with Roses and Raspberries

Gâteau Saint-Honoré is a French pastry named for the patron saint of bakers, pastry chefs, and confectioners. It's an elaborate cake made with a puff pastry base that's topped with little cream puffs, filled with pastry cream, and decorated with anything from caramel to fresh fruit and candied flowers. At Ladurée tea shops (see A Traveler's Guide to European Tearooms), you can buy a whole cake or enjoy individual ones like these with rose-flavored pastry cream, rose-infused fondant, and fresh raspberries.

1 sheet frozen puff pastry (from a 17-ounce package), such as Pepperidge Farm brand

½ recipe Choux Paste (see page 152)

ROSE CREAM

3 cups Crème Pâtissière (see page 94)

2 tablespoons rose water (see Resources, page 172)

2 cups whipped cream

ROSE FONDANT

¼ cup water

1 tablespoon light corn syrup

2 tablespoons rose water

3 cups confectioners' sugar

32 fresh raspberries

Preheat the oven to 400°F. Line 2 baking sheets with parchment paper.

Thaw the pastry at room temperature for 40 minutes. Unfold on a lightly floured surface and roll out into a ⅛-inch-thick sheet. With a 3½-inch biscuit cutter, cut out 8 rounds. With a fork, prick the surface all over to prevent excessive rising. Place the rounds on one of the prepared baking sheets. With a pastry bag fitted with a ½-inch plain tip, pipe a ring of choux paste

continued

around the outside edge of each pastry round. Pipe a second ring inside the first ring. On the second prepared baking sheet, pipe 24 small puffs of choux paste. Bake the small puffs for 22 to 28 minutes and the circular pastries about 10 minutes more, or until lightly puffed and browned. Remove from the oven and let cool.

TO MAKE THE CREAM Whip the *crème pâtissière* with the rose water, then fold in the whipped cream. Set aside.

TO MAKE THE FONDANT In a small saucepan over medium heat, combine the water, corn syrup, and rose water. Cook for 4 to 5 minutes, or until the mixture starts to thicken. Stir in the sugar and cook for 8 to 10 minutes, or until the temperature reaches 95°F on a candy thermometer. The fondant should be thin enough to be poured but thick enough to glaze. (Leftover fondant can be stored, covered, in the refrigerator for up to 3 weeks. To use again, reheat over medium heat to pouring consistency.)

Cover the top of each circular pastry with fondant. Immediately place 3 of the small puffs around the edge of the pastry (space them evenly) and cover each with the fondant. With a pastry bag fitted with a ½-inch fluted tip, decoratively pipe the rose cream between the small puffs and over the top. Insert a raspberry between the cream and each small puff and center one on top.

MAKES 8 INDIVIDUAL CAKES

THE POPULARITY of afternoon tea truly has no bounds. Elegant hotel dining rooms, quaint teashops, and ornate *salons de thé* provide the expected settings for the afternoon ritual, but luxury trains and cruise lines have also embraced the practice. Several Orient-Express Pullman trains—the Venice-Simplon Orient Express, which travels between Venice and Paris; the Royal Scotsman, which journeys through Scotland from April to October; and the British Pullman, which provides glamorous day excursions from London to various destinations in the English countryside—host afternoon tea services as soon as guests are on board. After enjoying Kir Royale or Champagne, travelers on British Pullman trains are presented with their own tiered tea stand stacked with small sandwiches, strawberry roulade, chocolate and hazelnut brownies, and a wide selection of teas. On board the Royal Scotsman, guests enjoy afternoon tea shortly after departing Edinburgh en route to one of four distinctive destinations in Scotland. Classic Scottish sweets include Dundee cake, sticky toffee pudding, and shortbread.

The ships of Crystal Cruise Lines also offer daily afternoon teatime aboard *Symphony* and *Serenity*. Set in the sunlit Palm Court, tea is served amid lush greenery, rattan furnishings, and soothing classical music. During the sailings, three themed teas are offered: a white-tie-and-tails English Colonial High Tea, with finger sandwiches, scones, and traditional pastries; American Summer Tea, with sandwiches, cheesecakes, apple cinnamon cupcakes, and an ice cream bar; and the very popular Mozart Tea, with traditional Tyrolean sandwiches and Austrian pastries ranging from Black Forest cake and kugelhopf to Dobos torte and Esterhazy slice. Staff dressed in velvet, brocade, and lace also offer specialty drinks such as *Kapuziner* (coffee with whipped cream and coffee powder), iced Vienna coffee, and hot chocolate "Amadeus" (with dark rum, whipped cream, and chocolate shavings). Yum!

Spiced Chocolate Cream

In case you haven't noticed, the French love chocolate—from *pains au chocolat* at breakfast to the most indulgent chocolate pastries for dessert. At Le Jardin d'Hiver at Hôtel Le Meurice (228 Rue de Rivoli), the chef serves marbled vanilla-chocolate cakes, chocolate fondants, and seasonal tarts at teatime, and even offers *chocolat chaud* (hot chocolate) in three strengths for those who really can't get enough. Try this delicious cup of rich chocolate cream with Chocolate Madeleines (page 142).

1 cup milk	3 star anise (see Note)
1 cup heavy whipping cream	5 ounces chocolate (preferably with
2 teaspoons sugar	70 percent cocoa), finely grated
3 cinnamon sticks	

In a medium saucepan over medium heat, combine the milk, cream, sugar, cinnamon sticks, and star anise. Cook for 4 to 5 minutes, or until the mixture starts to bubble but doesn't boil. Stir in the grated chocolate until melted. Remove the cinnamon sticks and star anise. Pour the mixture into eight 3-ounce espresso cups or cordial glasses. Refrigerate for 2 to 3 hours.

To serve, put a cup of spiced cream on a saucer or serving plate and serve with madeleines, if desired.

SERVES 8

NOTE Star anise is one of the spices in Chinese five-spice powder. You can find packages of the star-shaped, licorice-flavored seedpod in Asian supermarkets and some specialty grocery stores.

Crème Caramel Saint-Petersburg

Kusmi Tea, a company that originated in St. Petersburg, Russia, in 1867, was originally called P.M. Kousmichoff Tea House after its founder. By 1917 the tea company had no less than fifty-one tea boutiques throughout Russia. When the Russian Revolution broke out, the company moved its headquarters to Paris, shortened the company name to Kusmi, and expanded to Berlin, Hamburg, and other European capitals. Today there are two tea shops in Paris (75 Avenue Niel and 56 Rue de Seine), and its teas are distributed in international destinations such as Canada, Denmark, Japan, and the United States (see Resources, page 171). Many interesting recipes have been developed using Kusmi tea, including these delicious custards from Canadian chefs Christopher Alary and Pierre Watters.

CARAMEL	CUSTARD
⅓ cup sugar	1½ cups heavy whipping cream
⅓ cup water	½ cup milk
1 tablespoon Kusmi St. Petersburg Tea (see Note)	½ cup sugar
	1½ teaspoons Kusmi Christmas Tea (see Note)
	3 large eggs
	Madeleines (page 141) for serving (optional)

TO MAKE THE CARAMEL In a small saucepan over medium-high heat, combine the sugar, water, and tea. Cook for 4 to 6 minutes, tilting the pan occasionally, or until the sugar begins to caramelize and thicken. Pour immediately into six 4-ounce ramekins. Let cool for about 2 minutes.

continued

TO MAKE THE CUSTARD Preheat the oven to 325°F. In a medium saucepan over medium-high heat, combine the cream, milk, ¼ cup of the sugar, and the tea. Cook for 3 to 4 minutes, or until the milk is scalded (small bubbles will form around the side of the pan). Remove the pan from the heat and let sit for about 5 minutes to infuse. Strain the liquid into a clean bowl, then return the mixture to the saucepan over medium heat.

In a medium bowl, whisk the eggs with the remaining ¼ cup sugar. Slowly pour a little of the infused cream into the egg mixture, then gradually whisk it back into the hot cream. Cook, whisking frequently, for about 5 minutes, or until the mixture thickens.

Spoon the custard into the ramekins over the caramel and transfer to a baking pan. Add enough hot water to the pan to come halfway up the sides of the ramekins. Bake for 35 to 40 minutes, or until the custard is just set. Remove from the oven. Using tongs as an aid, remove the ramekins from the water bath. Let cool and wrap them in plastic wrap. Refrigerate for about 12 hours, or until chilled.

Run a knife around the sides of the ramekins and turn the crèmes out onto serving plates. Serve with madeleines, if desired.

SERVES 6

NOTE St. Petersburg Tea is a blend of China black teas flavored with citrus, red fruits, and caramel. It was created to celebrate the tercentennial of the city of St. Petersburg. Christmas Tea, also known as *Rois Mages*, is a blend of China black teas flavored with orange, almond, vanilla extract, and spices.

CHAPTER SIX

A Traveler's Guide
to European Tearooms

Still Too Few, a tearoom at 300 Westbourne Grove off of Portobello Road, is popular with Londoners and tourists who visit the Saturday street market there.

I have the simplest of tastes;
I am always satisfied with the best.

OSCAR WILDE, IRISH PLAYWRIGHT

ENGLAND

Athenaeum Hotel 116 Piccadilly, London
*(44-20-7499-3464, www.athenaeumhotel
.com)*. Afternoon tea is served from 2 to
6 P.M. daily; reservations suggested.

The Berkeley Wilton Place, Knightsbridge,
London *(44-20-7235-6000;
www.the-berkeley.co.uk)*. Prêt-à-Portea is
served in the Caramel Room from 2 to
6 P.M. daily; reservations suggested.

Bramah Museum of Tea and Coffee
40 Southwark Street, London *(44-20-7403-
5650, www.teaandcoffeemuseum.co.uk)*.
Serves lunch and afternoon tea in a space
adjacent to its museum of tea and coffee.
Shop hours vary.

Brown's Hotel Albemarle Street, London
(44-20-7493-6020, www.brownshotel.com).
Afternoon tea is served in the English
Tearoom from 3 to 6 P.M. weekdays;
from 2 to 6 P.M. weekends; reservations
suggested.

Claridge's Hotel Brook Street, London
(44-20-7409-6307, www.claridges.co.uk).
Afternoon tea is served in the Foyer from
3 to 5:30 P.M. daily; reservations required.

The Chesterfield Mayfair 35 Charles Street,
London *(44-20-7491-2622,
www.chesterfieldmayfair.com)*. Afternoon
tea is served in the Conservatory from
2:30 to 5:30 P.M. daily; reservations not
required.

The Dorchester Hotel Park Lane, London
(44-20-7629-8888, www.thedorchester.com).
Afternoon tea is served in the Promenade
from 2 to 5 P.M. daily; reservations
suggested.

The Four Seasons Hotel Hamilton Place,
Park Lane, London *(44-20-7499-0888,
www.fourseasons.com/london)*. Afternoon
tea is served in the Lounge from 3 to
7 P.M. daily; reservations suggested.

The Grove Chandler's Cross, Hertfordshire
(44-19-2329-6015, www.thegrove.co.uk).
Afternoon tea is served in the Lounge from
3 to 7 P.M. daily; reservations not required.

Ladurée at Harrods and at Burlington Arcade 87–135 Brompton Road, London *(44-20-3155-0111)*; 71–72 Burlington Arcade, London *(44-20-7491-9155; www.laduree.com)*. Shop hours vary.

Mandeville Hotel Mandeville Place, London *(44-20-7935-5599, www.mandeville.co.uk)*. Afternoon tea is served in the deVille Restaurant, Monday to Saturday from 3 to 5:30 P.M.; reservations suggested.

The Milestone Hotel and Apartments 1 Kensington Court, London *(44-20-7917-1000; www.milestonehotel.com)*. Afternoon tea is served from 2 to 5 P.M. daily in the Park Lounge; reservations suggested.

Peacocks Tea Room 68 Waterside, Ely, Cambridgeshire *(44-13-5366-1100, www.peacockstearoom.co.uk)*. The tearoom is open Wednesday to Sunday until 5 P.M.

The Ritz Hotel 150 Piccadilly, London *(44-20-7493-8181, www.theritzlondon.com)*. Afternoon tea is served in the Palm Court in five seatings from 11:30 A.M. to 7:30 P.M. daily; reservations recommended up to six weeks in advance.

The Savoy Strand, London *(44-20-7836-4343, www.fairmont.com/savoy)*. Afternoon tea is served Monday to Friday from 2 to 3:30 P.M. and from 4 to 5:30 P.M.; three seatings on weekends; reservations suggested.

Twinings Tea Shop 216 Strand, London *(44-20-7353-3511, www.twinings.com)*. Sells a wide range of specialty teas, fruit and herbal infusions, teas, and coffee blends. The shop also has a small museum that charts the history of the Twinings family, with examples of tea caddies and unusual items from the world of tea. Shop hours vary.

For general information on travel to England, visit www.visitbritain.com.

IRELAND

Adare Manor Hotel Adare, County Limerick (*353-61-605200, www.adaremanor.com*). Afternoon tea is served in the Drawing Room from 2:30 to 5 P.M. daily; reservations not required.

Ashford Castle Cong, County Mayo (*353-94-954-6003, www.ashford.ie*). Afternoon tea is served in the Drawing Room from 3 to 5 P.M. daily; reservations not required.

The Clarence Hotel 6–8 Wellington Quay, Dublin (*353-1-407-0813, www.theclarence.ie*). Afternoon tea is served in the Tea Room from 2 to 5 P.M. daily; reservations suggested.

Dromoland Castle Newmarket-on-Fergus, County Clare (*353-61-368144, www.dromoland.ie*). Afternoon tea is served in the Fig Tree Restaurant from 3 to 5 P.M. daily; reservations not required.

The Four Seasons Hotel Simmonscourt Road, Dublin (*353-1-665-4000, www.fourseasonshotels.com/dublin*). Afternoon tea is served in the Lobby Lounge from 3 to 5 P.M. daily; reservations suggested.

The Merrion Hotel Upper Merrion Street, Dublin (*353-603-0600, www.merrionhotel.com*). Afternoon tea is served in the Drawing Room from 3 to 5 P.M. daily; reservations suggested.

Park Hotel Kenmare, Kenmare, County Kerry (*353-64-41200, www.parkkenmare.com*). Informal afternoon tea is served daily in the Sitting Room.

Quay House Beach Road, Clifden (*353-95-21369, www.thequayhouse.com*). Informal afternoon tea is served daily in the Sitting Room.

Ritz-Carlton at Powerscourt Estate Enniskerry, County Wicklow (*353-1-274-8888, www.ritz-carlton.com*). Afternoon tea is served daily in the Sugar Loaf Lounge; reservations suggested.

Shelbourne Hotel 27 Stephen's Green, Dublin *(353-1-663-4500, www.marriott .co.uk)*. Afternoon tea is served daily in the Lord Mayor's Lounge; reservations not required.

The Westin Westmoreland Street, Dublin *(353-01-645-1000, www.westin.com/dublin)*. Afternoon tea is served in the Atrium from 3 to 5 P.M. daily; reservations suggested.

For general information on travel to Ireland, visit www.tourismireland.com.

PARIS

Ladurée 75 avenue des Champs Elysées; 16 rue Royale; 21 rue Bonaparte; Au Grande Magasin du Printemps, 62 boulevard Haussmann *(www.laduree .com)*. Shop hours vary.

Hôtel Le Bristol 112 rue du Faubourg Saint-Honoré *(33-1-53434300, www.hotel-bristol .com)*. Afternoon tea is served from 3:30 to 5 P.M. and special Fashion Teas are served monthly; reservations required.

Hôtel de Crillon 10 place de la Concorde *(33-1-44711500, www.crillon.com)*. Afternoon tea is served in the Jardin d'Hiver from 3 to 6 P.M. daily; reservations recommended.

Kusmi Tea Shops 75 avenue Niel and 56 rue de Seine *(www.kusmitea.com)*. Shop hours vary.

Le Meurice Hôtel 228 rue de Rivoli *(33-1-44581010, www.lemeurice.com)*. Afternoon tea is served in the Jardin d'Hiver from 3 to 6 P.M. daily; reservations recommended.

Mariage Frères 30 rue du Bourg-Tibourg; 13 rue des Grands-Augustins; 260 rue du Faubourg Saint-Honoré *(www .mariagefreres.com)*. Shop hours vary.

Pierre Hermé 72 rue Bonaparte; 185 rue du Vaugirard *(www.pierreherme.com)*. Shop hours vary.

Ritz Hôtel 15 Place Vendôme
(*33-1-43-163030, www.ritzparis.com*).
Afternoon tea is served in Bar Vendôme
from 3 to 5 P.M. daily; reservations
recommended.

For general information on travel to Paris,
visit www.parisinfo.com.

SCOTLAND

Balmoral Hotel 1 Princes Street, Edinburgh
(*44-131-556-2414, www.thebalmoralhotel
.com*). Afternoon tea is served in the
Bollinger Bar at the Palm Court from
2:30 to 4:30 P.M. daily; reservations
suggested.

Caledonian Hotel Princes Street, Edinburgh
(*44-131-222-8888, www.hilton.co.uk/
caledonian*). Afternoon tea is served in the
Castle Suite Lounge from 3 to 5:30 P.M.
daily; reservations suggested.

The Howard 34 Great King Street,
Edinburgh (*44-131-557-3500, www.the
howard.com*). Afternoon tea is served in

the Drawing Room from 2 to 5 P.M. daily;
reservations suggested.

Kinloch Lodge Sleat, Isle of Skye
(*44-1471-833214, www.kinloch-lodge.co.uk*).
Informal afternoon tea is served daily.

The Royal Scotsman is a luxury train
operated by the Great Scottish & Western
Railway Company Ltd. It is part of Orient-
Express Hotels, Trains, and Cruises and
offers a variety of itineraries through the
Scottish countryside in journeys ranging
from one to five nights (*1-800-524-2420,
www.royalscotsman.com or
www.orient-express.com*).

The Willow Tea Rooms 217 Sauchiehall
Street (*44-141-332-0521*) and
97 Buchanan Street (*44-141-204-5242*),
Glasgow; (*www.willowtearooms.co.uk*).
Afternoon tea is served all day.

For general information on travel to
Scotland, visit www.visitscotland.com.

SWITZERLAND

Hôtel d'Angleterre 17 Quai de Mont-Blanc, Geneva *(41-22-906-5555, www.dangleterrehotel.com)*. Afternoon tea is served from 2:30 to 5 P.M. daily in Windows Restaurant overlooking Lake Geneva; reservations suggested.

Ladurée 7 Cours de Rive, Geneva *(41-22-310-4404)*; 3 rue de Bourg, Lausanne *(41-21-312-7900, www.laduree.com)*. Shop hours vary.

For general information on travel to Switzerland, visit www.myswitzerland.com.

WALES

Bodysgallen Hall Llandudno, North Wales *(44-1492-584466, www.bodysgallen.com)*. Afternoon tea is served daily; reservations not required.

The Cawdor Hotel Rhosmaen Street, Llandeilo *(44-1558-823500, www.thecawdor.com)*. Afternoon tea is served daily; reservations not required.

Lake Country House Hotel Llangammarch Wells, Powys *(44-1591-620202, www.lakecountryhouse.com)*. Afternoon tea is served daily; reservations not required.

Llangoed Hall Llyswen, Brecon *(44-1874-754525, www.llangoedhall.com)*. Afternoon tea is served daily; reservations not required.

Morgans Somerset Place, Swansea *(44-1792-484848, www.morganshotel.co.uk)*. Afternoon tea is served daily; reservations not required.

For general information on travel to Wales, visit www.visitwales.com.

Resources

Use this guide to find ingredients and equipment called for in some recipes and for information on other tea-related items.

ALMOND PASTE

Almond paste is made of ground almonds, sugar, and glucose and is used as a filling in a number of baked goods. Odense almond paste, imported by Andre Prost Company, is a popular brand. It's available in the baking aisle of most supermarkets. To find a store where it's sold, visit www.odense.com.

BUNDT PANS

Nordic Ware is a manufacturer of quality cookware and bakeware products and is best known for creating the Original Bundt Pan. To view the complete line of products, visit them online at www.nordicware.com.

CARR'S DIGESTIVE BISCUITS

These oaty biscuits can generally be found in the cookie and cracker section of most supermarkets.

CHOCOLATE CUPS AND SHELLS

Astor Chocolate makes fluted chocolate shells (seashell, round, and square shaped) and chocolate liqueur cups for filling with mousse and flavored whipped creams. To locate a store near you that sells them, visit www.astorchocolates.com.

CHUTNEY

Major Grey's is a popular type of mango chutney found in the condiments section of most supermarkets. The most popular brand of Major Grey's chutney is Crosse & Blackwell.

CLOTTED CREAM

Clotted cream is a thick yellow cream used as a spread on scones. Originating in the southwest English counties of Devon and Cornwall, it's available in some specialty food stores or online at www.englishtea store.com; www.britishdelights.com; and www.bakerscatalogue.com.

CRÈME FRAÎCHE

Commercially made crème fraîche is available in the dairy case of most supermarkets. One brand to look for is Vermont Butter and Cheese, a company that crafts artisanal dairy products in the European style. To locate a store near you that sells its products, visit www.vtbutterandcheese.com.

CRUMPETS

You can buy British-style toaster crumpets in the dairy case at your local supermarket. Gourmet Baker brand, from Multifoods, St. Paul, Minnesota, is one brand to look for.

CRUMPET RINGS

Also called English muffin rings, crumpet rings are available at some gourmet stores or online from Sur La Table at www.surlatable .com. One brand to look for is Norpro, a company that sells the rings in boxes of four.

GOOSEBERRIES

You can find jars of gooseberries in syrup in some specialty grocery stores, especially those carrying German products. Two brands to look for are Vavel and Landsberg.

KUSMI TEA

Kusmi Tea, a company that originated in St. Petersburg, Russia, was originally called P. M. Kousmichoff Tea House after its founder. When the Russian Revolution broke out, the company moved its headquarters to Paris, where it now operates tea shops and tearooms. To order Kusmi tea online, visit www.kusmitea.com.

MARZIPAN

Marzipan is made with ground almonds, sugar, and glucose and is generally used for making candy or decorations for baked goods. It's milled to a smoother consistency than almond paste, making it more pliable for rolling out and modeling. Odense brand, imported by Andre Prost Company, is a popular brand. It's available in the baking section of most supermarkets. To find a store where it's sold, visit www.odense.com.

MCVITIE'S HOBNOBS

These English cookies can be found in the foreign foods section of most supermarkets.

MUSCOVADO SUGAR

Muscovado sugar, also known as Barbados or moist sugar, is a type of unrefined sugar with a strong molasses flavor. You can order it from the Baker's Catalogue. Visit www.kingarthurflour.com or www.bakers catalogue.com.

PHYLLO SHELLS

Athens brand makes frozen phyllo (fillo) tart shells that can be used for savory and sweet fillings. The shells are sold in packages of fifteen and are available in the frozen food section of most supermarkets. For more on Athens, visit them online at www.athens.com.

RACHEL GAFFNEYS SHORTBREAD

To find a store near you that sells Rachel Gaffney's Shortbread, visit www.rachel gaffney.com.

ROSE WATER

Rose water is generally made from the flowers of the damask rose and is often used in Middle Eastern cooking and baking. You can order it from Spice House, an Illinois-based purveyor of spices, herbs, and seasonings. Visit www.spicehouse.com or phone 312-274-0378.

SCONE PANS

King Arthur Flour, based in Norwich, Vermont, is America's oldest flour company. It publishes Baker's Catalogue, a one-stop shop for baking needs including many varieties of flour, sugars, spices, condiments, and scone pans. Visit www.kingarthurflour .com or www.bakerscatalogue.com.

SEMOLINA FLOUR

Sometimes called "pasta flour," semolina is made from durum wheat that is more coarsely ground than normal wheat flour. It adds a grainy texture to shortbread.

SUGAR CRYSTALS

Bright-white, irregular Swedish pearl sugar crystals don't melt on cookies or scones. You can order decorating sugars like this from the Baker's Catalogue. Visit www.kingarthurflour.com or www.bakers catalogue.com.

SUR LA TABLE

Sur la Table is a specialty retailer of food and kitchenware. Its products are sold in retail stores, by catalogue, and over the Internet. Visit them online at www.surlatable.com.

TART SHELLS

Clearbrook Farms Bakehouse sweet tart shells are prebaked shortbread shells that can be filled with prepared fruit preserves, lemon curd, custard, or fresh fruit. The shells can also be filled with a homemade filling and baked. They're available in boxes of twelve regular size and twenty-four miniature. To locate a store near you that sells them, or to order them online, visit www.clearbrookfarms.com.

TWININGS

Twinings is the world's leading brand of premium tea. Its tea is available worldwide in shops and supermarkets and at its original London location at 216 Strand. For more on Twinings, visit them online at www.twinings.com.

WALKERS SHORTBREAD

Walkers, established in 1898 in the Scottish village of Aberlour-on-Spey, is the oldest shortbread company in the world. Its shortbread, oatcakes, biscuits, and fruit breads are widely available in supermarkets. For more on Walkers, visit them online at www.walkersshortbread.com.

WILLIAMS-SONOMA

Founded in 1956, Williams-Sonoma is a specialty retailer of home furnishings and kitchenware. Its products are sold in retail stores, by catalogue, and over the Internet. For more on Williams-Sonoma, visit them online at www.williams-sonoma.com.

Index

Tea at the Ritz, London, takes place in five seatings daily with offerings presented on a three-tiered serving stand.

Table of Equivalents

The exact equivalents in the following tables have been rounded for convenience.

LIQUID/DRY MEASUREMENTS

U.S	METRIC
¼ teaspoon	1.25 milliliters
½ teaspoon	2.5 milliliters
1 teaspoon	5 milliliters
1 tablespoon (3 teaspoons)	15 milliliters
1 fluid ounce (2 tablespoons)	30 milliliters
¼ cup	60 milliliters
⅓ cup	80 milliliters
½ cup	120 milliliters
1 cup	240 milliliters
1 pint (2 cups)	480 milliliters
1 quart (4 cups, 32 ounces)	960 milliliters
1 gallon (4 quarts)	3.84 liters
1 ounce (by weight)	28 grams
1 pound	448 grams
2.2 pounds	1 kilogram

LENGTHS

U.S.	METRIC
⅛ inch	3 millimeters
¼ inch	6 millimeters
½ inch	12 millimeters
1 inch	2.5 centimeters

OVEN TEMPERATURES

FAHRENHEIT	CELSIUS	GAS
250	120	½
275	140	1
300	150	2
325	160	3
350	180	4
375	190	5
400	200	6
425	220	7
450	230	8
475	240	9
500	260	10